Why Spirituality is Difficult for Westerners

David Hay

SOCIETAS
essays in political
& cultural criticism

imprint-academic.com

Published in the UK by Societas
Imprint Academic, PO Box 200, Exeter EX5 5YX, UK

Published in the USA by Societas
Imprint Academic, Philosophy Documentation Center
PO Box 7147, Charlottesville, VA 22906-7147, USA

ISBN 9781845400484

A CIP catalogue record for this book is available from the
British Library and US Library of Congress

Contents

FOR SIMON

Preface

After a lengthy period in the doldrums, religion is on the public agenda again. Who could have guessed ahead of time that during the opening decade of the 21st century a 400 page polemical attack on religion would be at or near the top of the best-seller lists on both sides of the Atlantic for many weeks? And Richard Dawkins' furious denunciation of theism in *The God Delusion*, published in 2006, is only the most celebrated of a whole series of secularist broadsides delivered so closely together that they might almost belong to a coordinated campaign.

Why now? The explanations bandied about include the suggestion that they are responses to the fear catalysed by a chain of spectacular attacks on Western targets by terrorists claiming to represent Islam. Another source of anxiety is the rise to political power of Christian Fundamentalism in parts of the United States, bringing with it the possibility of the reversal of liberal policies at both state and federal level, as in the ongoing controversy over the teaching of Creationism in schools. A third, rather more paranoid speculation interprets the concerted attack on religion as an attempted *coupe de grace* timed to coincide with a period when the mainstream Christian institutions in large sections of the Western world are in a state of low morale with rapidly falling congregations, chronic shortage of clergy and persistent sex scandals.

I do not deny that any of these factors may have played an important part in stirring up the current assault on religion, but I believe that there is another deeper reason for the critique. The English sociologist Grace Davie has recently

reminded us that in matters of religion Europe is an exceptional case.[1] For many Europeans the default assumption
about human nature is that we are born atheists who come
to subscribe to a specific faith through socialisation into a
religious culture. In my view the empirical evidence that
has been accumulating over the past thirty years casts doubt
on that assumption.

In this short book I argue the opposite case. Human
beings appear to be born with an inbuilt spiritual awareness
that in normal circumstances expresses itself via the religious culture in which we are nurtured. The closest analogy
is with Noam Chomsky's language acquisition device
(LAD) that is biologically structured into us and comes to
fruition in the multitude of languages that are our cultural
inheritance. I suggest that like the LAD, spiritual awareness
is a human universal, part of our biological make up that
has evolved through the process of natural selection
because it has survival value.

The first person to put this view forward in explicitly biological terms was Professor Sir Alister Hardy FRS, at one
time head of the Zoology Department in Oxford University
and founder of the Religious Experience Research Unit in
Manchester College, Oxford in 1969. I met Hardy in the
1950s when I was an undergraduate reading zoology at
Aberdeen University, which is where he gave the first
extended treatment to the conjecture in his Gifford Lectures
in 1963–4 and 1964–5. I began working with Hardy's Unit in
1974, taking over as director in 1985, the year he died. Consequently I have been investigating these matters for most
of my professional life and have come to the conclusion that
the empirical evidence strongly supports the hypothesis.

In spite of my conclusion, the biological argument has
had problems of plausibility within the academic community because it contradicts major assumptions — one might
almost class them as axioms about the nature of reality —
drawn from the mainstream of the European Enlighten-
ment. The discrepancy has dictated the structure of the

---

[1]   See *Europe: The Special Case* (Darton, Longman & Todd, 2002).

argument in this book, which is divided into four chapters. I open with an account of the practical nature of religion and a summary of the research that led to the proposal that the primordial basis for both religion and ethics is 'relational consciousness'. In the second chapter I offer evidence of the longstanding dislike and suspicion of religion in Europe and how this currently expresses itself in the reductionism of a number of scientist critics who are inclined to classify religious belief as a disease. The pivot of my argument is in Chapter 3 where I outline the social construction of scepticism in Europe and how it has led to a covering over or repression of our natural spirituality. In the final chapter I present the most recent empirical evidence that leads to a rejection of the secularist hypothesis, along with reasons to expect a greater openness to spiritual awareness in the future.

There is more to my argument than an attempt to get at the scientific truth underlying our spiritual awareness, for I believe that many of our most pressing social and political problems — meaninglessness, the collapse of a sense of human community, the draining away of trust and social capital in general, the turning of everything into a commodity, and carelessness about the ecology of our planet – have their origin in the ignoring of the aspect of our human nature adapted to deal with them, relational consciousness or spirituality.

It is here that the religious institutions, with all their chronic weaknesses are still the best-equipped bodies to give leadership. I see no adequate substitute for them though they will have to adapt radically if they are to recover their role as our major repositories of spiritual wisdom. We are in profound territory here, where language often fails us and we are in danger of sounding ridiculous, as Richard Dawkins cuttingly remarks in his comments on religious doctrines. As a committed religious believer, I nevertheless on occasion find myself not too far away from the view of the founding father of the scientific investigation of spiritual experience, William James. In a letter to his friend Frances Morse he writes about the motivation behind his Gifford lectures on religious experience, delivered in Edinburgh University in 1901 and 1902:

> ... I invincibly do believe, that, although all the special manifestations of religion may have been absurd (I mean its creeds and theories), yet the life of it as a whole is mankind's most important function.[2]

This monograph was written whilst I was the holder of an honorary Senior Research Fellowship in the Divinity and Religious Studies Department in my *alma mater*. I am delighted to have had the opportunity to return to my first academic home. In particular I am grateful to Professor John Swinton for his enthusiastic support, his searching questions about the development of my ideas on the subject of spirituality, and for his friendship.

David Hay
King's College
Aberdeen University

---

[2]   From *The Letters of William James*, ed. Henry James (Little, Brown & Co: Boston, 1920). See, Vol. I, 127. See also *The Varieties of Religious Experience*, the published version of the lectures. The most authoritative edition, including a complete scholarly apparatus, is that published by Harvard University Press in 1985.

Chapter One

Doing Religion

'We don't do religion!'[1]

Empirical Religion

I'd been going through a spell when too many things were
going wrong in my life and I'd come to this place to do
something about it. As I made my way along the corridor it
felt like the middle of a winter's night and I was tensing my
body against the cold. In the gloom, apart from my own
breathing the only sounds I could hear were soft footsteps
and the rustle of my companions' clothing. On reaching the
chapel I entered with slow deliberation, grateful for the sud-
den warmth, found the place that felt right for me and
waited in silence. A bell intoned once and the sound spun
through the air, fading down to a nothingness where there
is no 'was' or 'will be', only the single point of 'now'. My
purpose is to attend to this 'now' with as much heart and
soul and mind and strength as I can muster.

Like most people who try this kind of thing, at first my
efforts are sporadic and my awareness is all over the place,
filled with a jumble of thoughts, hopes, anxieties and
despairs, erotic longings, bodily aches and involuntary
twitches, snatches of music, dreams … On a lucky night,
and quite distinct from my stumbling efforts, I experience a
presence or a given force gradually taking over and
catalysing the dropping away of the chatter. Beyond or
within, or above the complexity (who knows where?)

---

[1] Tony Blair's press spokesman Alastair Campbell's remark when asked
about Blair's beliefs.

—there is an encounter, immensely vivid, in which I am addressed. By analogy with music, the discord I've been feeling is resolving and I'm coming back into tune, able to handle the situation in a way that didn't seem possible an hour ago. I am filled with gratitude. But these are mere words. Words are a constriction, categorizing what transcends every conceivable category, dragging down to their size the manifold reality in which we live and move and have our being. These patterns of words, these doctrines, are no more than a sample of the semi-coherent responses of a multitude of religious cultures to the experience of transcendence, and they are simultaneously marvellous and inadequate.

I have been immersed since my birth in one or other version of the European rejoinder to what Rudolf Otto[2] calls the *mysterium tremendum*. To be more specific as to the episode in the chapel, it is a memory of time spent in St Beuno's College, the Jesuit house in the hills of North Wales where Gerard Manley Hopkins came in 1874 to study for the priesthood and where he wrote some of his finest poetry. When I reach out as best I can for language appropriate to my experience of prayer it is natural enough to call upon Hopkins, who in turn draws from the same well as myself, sometimes in great delight:

> Wild air, world-mothering air,
> Nestling me everywhere,
> That each eyelash or hair
> Girdles; goes home betwixt
> The fleeciest, frailest-flixed
> Snowflake ...
>
> I say that we are wound
> With mercy round and round
> As if with air...[3]

At other times in an anguish of alienation:

---

[2]   See, *The Idea of the Holy*, trans. J.W. Harvey (Oxford University Press, 1950).

[3]   In, Gerald H. Gardner, *Gerard Manley Hopkins, A Selection of His Poems and Prose* (Harmondsworth: Penguin, 1953), pp. 54, 55. For an informative biography, see Robert Bernard Martin, *Gerard Manley Hopkins: a very private life* (New York: Putnam, 1991).

I wake and feel the fell of dark, not day.
What hours, O what black hours we have spent
This night! what sights you, heart saw, ways you went!
And more must in yet longer light's delay.
    With witness I speak this. But where I say
Hours I mean years, mean life.[4]

In times of consolation Hopkins found his own and others' spiritual *ennui* difficult to comprehend:

The world is charged with the grandeur of God
It will flame out, like shining from shook foil;
It gathers to a greatness, like the ooze of oil
Crushed. Why do men not now then reck his rod?[5]

For awareness of the presence of God is commonly accompanied by an embodied, physical longing for universal justice, given ecstatic utterance in the synagogue at Nazareth by Jesus, the culture hero to whom Hopkins dedicated his life:

The Spirit of the Lord has been given to me,
For he has anointed me,
He has sent me to bring good news to the poor,
To proclaim liberty to captives and to the blind new sight,
To set the downtrodden free,
To proclaim the Lord's year of favour.[6]

The Primordial Context of Religion

However inadequate my ongoing spiritual practice may be, occasions like my visit to St Beuno's have convinced me that the spiritual quest is authentic and prayer is its living heart. For me, contemplative prayer[7] has analogies with the experiment in empirical science. It is the practical investigation through which (and here language gives out once more) there is a discovery of meaning, of one's identity and the

---

[4]   W.H. Gardner, op.cit. p. 62
[5]   *Ibid.,* p. 27
[6]   This is a passage from Isaiah 61: 1-2, quoted by Jesus in the synagogue as reported in Luke 4: 18-19
[7]   I am using the term 'contemplative prayer' as a recognizable shorthand to distinguish it from petitionary prayer in which one asks for something. Technically speaking, contemplation in the Christian tradition refers to a stage in prayer when God's presence is infused and the prayer 'does itself'. Prior to that the hard work of attempting to stay in the presence of God is more correctly called the prayer of silence.

larger context of one's existence, the loss of alienation, of feeling at home in the universe.

Whilst the reality encountered in prayer is the very opposite of vague, the constraints of language to which I have just referred mean that definitions in this area *sound* vague and self-contradictory. Much of my professional life as a scientist has been spent in the investigation of spirituality and a few years ago I began to wonder if there might be a practical way of getting beyond the difficulty with language. The problem facing me was to find a working definition of spirituality that could be used as the key question in a large-scale national survey on the subject. One Summer I organized a seminar made up of philosophers, theologians and other specialists to try to pin down a form of words. The experts were hopelessly at odds with each other and in the end we gave up. However, I noticed that although the seminar was in that sense a failure, one point everyone agreed upon was that concrete examples of spiritual experience were recognisable when they saw them. There was also some common ground about the environmental triggers that were conducive to such experience. It seemed to me that this might offer a way to move forward pragmatically to some general statement about the primordial nature of spirituality, based on what ordinary people said about their experience.

The opportunity to investigate this question came during the 1990s when I managed to secure the funding to make a study of children's spirituality. Chastened by the problems of definition, I was fortunate to be joined in this task by a psychologist, Rebecca Nye, and together we took the first steps towards identifying some of the contexts that would likely be appropriate for the emergence of spiritual experience, if such a thing was a reality. We began by reflecting on our own devotional lives, particularly recalling those circumstances that seemed to be associated with instances of spontaneous spiritual awareness. More help came from examining the practical instructions in technical manuals of prayer and meditation, and also from reading the archive of more than 5000 accounts of first hand experience collected by Alister Hardy's Religious Experience Research Unit in Oxford.[8] In the end we came up with three major categories:

- *Awareness of the here-and-now.* We chose this because we saw it as central to the practice of all the major religious traditions known to us. This is most obvious in Eastern religions like Buddhism and the Hindu Vedanta where there is emphasis on 'single pointed' meditation. In the Theravadin *vipassana* or awareness meditation that I was taught many years ago by a Thai monk the aim is to give attention to the breathing in sitting meditation, or to the movements of the body during slow walking. Persevering with this attentiveness brings about a greatly increased intensity of perception leading eventually, if one is to take the masters of the discipline at their word, to an insight into ultimate reality. In view of my own experience of the striking impact of the initial stages of *vipassana*, I am inclined to trust the statements of those who have gone much further than I.[9]

  How does *vipassana* relate to the practices in theistic traditions, for example, to the prayer life of the devout Christian or Muslim? At first sight the intentions of someone praying to God seem fundamentally different from those of a meditator belonging to an atheist religion like Buddhism. In practice they are much closer than might be expected. Thus, contemplative prayer such as is advocated in a Christian classic like *The Cloud of Unknowing* [10]requires exactly the same intention to stay in 'this moment' although in this case it is with the purpose of

[8]   Hardy founded the Unit in Oxford in 1969, following the success of his Gifford Lectures in Aberdeen University. The Unit, now called the *Religious Experience Research Centre* is relocated in the University of Wales, Lampeter.

[9]   This requires trust in the integrity of statements of the masters of meditation when they talk of higher levels of attainment, well beyond one's personal experience. It is important to note that dependence on authority is just as salient in the world of empirical science, as attested by the rows of fat undergraduate text books of scientific theory that still line my shelves. In principle all factual assertions appearing in such texts are testable by the reader. In practice only a tiny fraction of them are ever checked in this way because of our human limitations of time and energy, but we normally accept what we read on the assumption that the originators of the evidence are honest (and of course they aren't always honest, either in science or religion).

[10]   This anonymous 14th century mystical work is thought to have been written in the English Midlands, possibly by a Carthusian monk. See Clifton Wolters' translation (Harmondsworth: Penguin Books, 1961).

remaining in the presence of God. The instructions in the *Cloud* include the advice to select a word or phrase like 'God' or 'love' and use it repeatedly as a means to call back the attention to the immediate here-and-now, somewhat like a mantra in Buddhism.

To maintain awareness of the here-and-now is to move into what psychologists call the 'point mode',[11] the form of awareness found in the newborn child, who as yet has no conscious access to the past or future. Critics point to this as an example of regression and evidence of the infantile nature of religion, a charge that originates in psychoanalysis. But psychoanalysts themselves have made the point that not all regression need necessarily be equated with childishness. In 1952 the psychoanalyst Ernst Kris in his book *Psychoanalytic Explorations in Art*[12] described the production of a work of art as 'regression in the service of the ego', an intentional return to an earlier form of awareness to allow the emergence of primordial creativity. Kris and others who have followed are making the point that such an intention is not a sign of pathology, but the mature use of a creative competence. The skills used in contemplative prayer are arguably to enable a similar intentional regression away from the 'line mode' characteristic of adult life, where the great majority of our time is spent in considering the past and future. To shift from the line mode into the mode of prayer or meditation is to open up a form of awareness that is normally closed off or at times repressed in adult life. In a later chapter I will discuss the role of European history in crippling this skill.

- *Awareness of mystery.* Secularist critics get testy about the use of words like 'mysterious' to refer to reality, seeing it as a cover for lazy thinking. But there is undeniably a profound mystery lying at the heart of existence. The kind of questions that sooner or later occur to everyone (in my experience they typically emerge when one is lying awake in the middle of the night) are 'Why is there something and not nothing?' and 'What is the identity of this

[11] See Margaret Donaldson's book *Human Minds: an Exploration* (London: Allen Lane, 1992).

[12] A new edition appeared in 1988, published in Madison, Connecticut by International Universities Press. For developments of Kris' approach, see, Richard D. Chessick, *Emotional Illness and Creativity: A Psychoanalytic and Phenomenologic Study* (Madison: International Universities Press, 1999).

being I call 'I' and which is arbitrarily assigned a name and nationality, a way of clothing the body, a culture - but as a 'given' is a naked anonymous physical presence without any of these attributes. The questions that begin in early childhood (enquiries about things like: Where does the sun go when it sets? Why is grass green? Why does the light go on when I switch the switch? Where was I before I was born?) are outriders of the existential questions. We learn important scientific answers to these questions as we proceed through the educational system and they are sufficiently interesting and practically useful to quell most of our existential curiosity. They preoccupy us and allow us to lose touch with the underlying strangeness, summarised by the German philosopher Martin Heidegger in *Sein und Zeit*[13] as 'forgetfulness of Being'.

Even after the demise of the logical positivism that was popular in the 1950s there remains a strong body of scientific opinion insisting that questions of superordinate meaning are in fact non-questions and that those who ask them are infantile, as suggested earlier. But to accept that there are such mysteries is not to glory in or wallow in ignorance.[14] Acceptance points to the way in which one can come to grips with them. The appropriate method is to observe intently, using a method very similar to that advocated by the great Harvard zoologist Louis Agassiz to his student Samuel Scudder.[15] The young student thought that after ten minutes examination of the fish given to him by Agassiz to study, he had seen all there was to see. After the three days of contemplation insisted upon by his teacher, Scudder began to see much more. Contemplation requires time, patience and the ability to wait, as vividly described in Simone Weil's essay *Waiting*

[13] Published in English translation as *Being and Time*, trans. John Macquarrie and Edward Robinson,) (Oxford: Basil Blackwell, 1962). Heidegger is notoriously hard going, especially for non-philosophers. Hubert Dreyfus' *Being in the* World, a commentary on Division One of *Being and Time* is a very helpful guide, (London and Cambridge, MA, 1991).

[14] Rather like someone I met recently who, having been to a public lecture by an eminent philosopher, remarked, 'It was wonderful; I didn't understand a word!'

[15] See, Samuel H. Scudder, 'Look at your fish', written in 1874 and republished in David A. Erlandson, Barbara L. Skipper, Edward L. Harris, *Doing Naturalistic Inquiry: A Guide to Methods* (Newbury Park, CA, & London: Sage Publications Inc., 1993), pp. 1–4

for God.[16] In that respect, Samuel Beckett was right to use the word 'waiting' in the title of his most famous play *Waiting for Godot*. But the mode of Vladimir and Estragon's waiting is a misguided effort, the restricted, blind and deaf waiting that characterises the sterile end point of a particular cultural trajectory in Europe.[17]

- *Awareness of value* – I have in one of my desk drawers a cheap watchstrap that I am unable to throw away because it belonged to my father. We say of such keepsakes that they have sentimental value; and authentic valuation is a matter of sentiment. Oscar Wilde has Lord Darlington in his play *Lady Windermere's Fan* give the definition of a cynic as 'someone who knows the price of everything and the value of nothing'. In a later chapter I shall be discussing the way that the commodification of all dimensions of life, including religion, turns the measure of value into how much something costs. In the Western religious tradition the archetypal critique of the pecuniary estimation of value is the story of the widow's mite:

  > He looked up and saw the rich putting their gifts into the treasury; and he saw a poor widow put in two copper coins. And he said, "Truly I tell you, this poor widow has put in more than all of them; for they all contributed out of their abundance, but she out of her poverty put in all the living that she had.[18]

  Financial common sense tells us that the widow's mite judged as the most valuable offering was 'in reality' worthless and no help. One's feeling of disgust at such economic realism is because natural values have nothing to do with money. It is also within this understanding of value that religion for the believer commonly has the highest of all values. Consequently one might expect spiritual awareness to be associated with situations where high valuations of this type were being made.

Having identified the three categories – *awareness of the here-and-now, awareness of mystery, awareness of value* – we then had to consider how to present them in the context of

[16]   Simone Weil, *Waiting for God* (London: HarperCollins, 2001).
[17]   See my book *Something There: The Biology Of The Human Spirit* (London: Darton, Longman & Todd, 2006 and Philadephia: Templeton Foundation Press, 2007).
[18]   Luke 21: 1–4

practical research, in this case an investigation of the spirituality of children aged six and ten years of age. The reasoning behind this choice was based on the prior assumption that in a highly secularised country like the United Kingdom, overt examples of spiritual experience should be most obvious in young children, since they have not yet been socialised into the belief that such things cannot happen. The accuracy of this view was born out by the results. We chose what is called a projective method. The children were shown photographs of young people of approximately the same age as themselves in situations where one might expect one or other of the three categories to be in operation. They were then asked to imagine what was happening in the photographs, on the presumption that the responses would correspond with what they, the questioned children would feel in those circumstances. Thus a picture of a boy looking at the stars might link with feelings of awe, or a photograph of a girl crying because her pet gerbil has died might evoke connections with existential questions about life and death. I summarise the findings here, but for more detail *The Spirit of the Child*, the book that I wrote with the help of Rebecca Nye, should be consulted.[19]

Relational Consciousness

The most important point is that all the children without exception were aware of a spiritual dimension to their experience. When the tape-recorded responses were transcribed and stored on a computer they were explored with the use of a piece of software (NUD•IST)[20] designed to help with the analysis of units of meaning in a text. NUD•IST can also be used to help in the identification of an overall meaningfulness within a collection of texts. Rebecca, who did the field work for the project, analysed over a thousand pages of transcribed conversation with children and summarised the concept that linked all the units of meaning as

[19] See David Hay with Rebecca Nye, *The Spirit of the Child* (revised edition) (London: Jessica Kingsley, 2006).

[20] See the *User's Guide* to QSR NUD•IST (London: Sage/SCOLARI, 1996).

relational consciousness. Relational consciousness has two components (a) an altered state of awareness as compared with other kinds of consciousness, more intense, more serious and more valued and (b) the experience of being in relationship — with other people, with the environment and with God, and in an important sense, in touch with oneself.

My hypothesis is that relational consciousness is a biologically inbuilt aspect of our psychology. In accordance with the proposal of the zoologist Alister Hardy in his Gifford Lectures[21] in Aberdeen University, I suggest that relational consciousness has been selected for in the process of organic evolution because it has survival value.

The conclusion that relational consciousness is the common feature of all spiritual talk raises the question of whether it would be appropriate to say that the two terms are synonymous; that spirituality is equivalent to relational consciousness. To do so is to alter the traditional meaning drastically by extending the connotation well beyond religious belief since the criterion is 'relationship' and not religion. Nevertheless the expansion of meaning opens a way to bridge the gulf between religious and secular stances with regard to transcendence. Furthermore, we can immediately see that any form of social construction that leads to an emphasis on the individual rather than the community within which the individual was nurtured is likely to be damaging to relational consciousness, or as I am now calling it, spiritual awareness. This point will become crucial when I discuss the role of European individualism in constricting the expression of relational consciousness.

A second result of reframing the meaning of spirituality in this way is the suggestion that as the primordial, biologically inbuilt basis of spirituality, relational consciousness is the underpinning of both religion and ethics:

The underpinning of religion. As the means by which the devout theist becomes directly aware of the relationship to God, relational consciousness permits the possibility of

---

[21] Published as *The Living Stream* (London: Collins, 1965) and *The Divine Flame* (London: Collins, 1966).

theistic religion. Within a different cultural tradition like Buddhism that is at the official level atheist and religious simultaneously, social construction directs the adherent's attention to the holistic dimension of awareness and the loss of separation. This leads to familiar assertions of the type '*atman* (approximately, the individual soul) and *Brahman* (universal reality) are identical', or as it is expressed in the Advaita Vedanta saying taken from the *Chandogya Upanishad* – *Tat Tvam Asi* – or, 'Thou art that'. Academic dissertations on fine distinctions in theology and in Buddhist or Vedanta a-theology often look like exercises in futility to practitioners within these religious traditions who seem to find common ground in spite of scholarly critique. Pragmatically, the distinction between theism and atheism cannot be too strictly drawn, since there are historical examples of adepts of contemplative prayer within the Christian tradition who found themselves moving towards monism. Probably the best known is the 14th century Dominican friar, Meister Eckhart, who got himself into trouble with the religious theoreticians of his day for seeming to suggest that in prayer the separation from God disappears, apart from a single point that enables the person to get back to themselves. The 16th century Spanish Carmelite mystic, John of the Cross, was similarly suspect. In his *Spiritual Letters* published in 1935, the Benedictine monk Dom John Chapman recalls John's near monism being dismissed by his abbot:

> The abbot says St John of the Cross is like a sponge full of Christianity. You can squeeze it all out, and the full mystical theory remains. Consequently for fifteen years or so I hated St John of the Cross and called him a Buddhist.[22]

On the other hand, whilst the austere Buddhism of the Theravada is officially atheist, folk Buddhism in its homelands expresses itself through the worship of a multitude of Gods. The ambivalence on this issue suggests that the human experience of the transcendent simply is ambiguous

---

[22] The *Spiritual Letters* (London: Sheed and Ward). The abbot referred to was Dom Columba Marmion. See p. 269

and orthodoxies that insist on one interpretation to the exclusion of the other are simplifying the complex reality. As we shall see in a later chapter, there may be a physiological reason for the ambiguity.

The underpinning of ethics. Relational consciousness can be plausibly thought of as the primordial, biological basis of ethics. I have come to this view from a consideration of the research evidence gathered over thirty years from many hundreds of people, talking about the effects of religious or spiritual experience on their subsequent lives. Almost without exception these people report that they wish to behave better. This can be expressed in a variety of ways, including an increased desire for social justice, a wish to be more careful of the environment, a loss of prejudices of various kinds (homophobia, racism, sexism etc.) and an increased interest in religious or spiritual matters. In attempting to summarise this, I would describe the effect of experience as shortening the psychological distance between the individual and their environment, so that damage to it, which had perhaps been hitherto a matter of indifference, now is of direct and personal importance. There is a new insight that injury to the people or places around one is also harm to oneself.

   This finding is supported by parallel research directed by Professor Andrew Greeley[23] at the National Opinion Research Center at the University of Chicago and by Professor Robert Wuthnow[24] at the University of California and subsequently in Princeton. The agreement between the researches cited is remarkable and suggests that it may based on more than socialisation (i.e. heredity; see Chapter 4), though of course the appropriate upbringing is of the greatest importance for the nurture of the relational consciousness that I am suggesting underlies ethical behaviour. There is a link too with the philosophical work of

---

[23] See, *The Sociology of the Paranormal: A Reconnaissance*. Sage Research Papers in the Social Sciences (Studies in Religion and Ethnicity Series No. 90–23), (Beverley Hills & London: Sage Publications, 1975).

[24] See, *The Consciousness Reformation* (Berkeley: University of California Press, 1975).

Martin Buber[25] on the distinction between relationships which have an 'I-Thou' quality, where there is intersubjective recognition of the dignity and value of the other person, and those that are based on 'I-It', where there is no such recognition and the other person is as it were, fair game, and legitimately open to manipulation for one's own gratification.

More recently than Buber, his fellow Jewish philosopher Emmanuel Levinas takes the nature of relationship a step further, in positing 'ethics as first philosophy'.[26] That is to say, before all discursive thought of any kind whether scientific, theological or philosophical, if I look attentively I find an imperative to care for the other person, which has a higher priority than my own needs, even to the extent of risking my life for that person. Levinas talks of the 'gaze' that opens up awareness of this obligation. Most of Levinas' family perished in the Nazi Holocaust, so this is a remarkably optimistic vision on his part. What, one might wonder, had happened to the gaze of the concentration camp guards who slaughtered Levinas' relatives? Levinas' response is that they have learned how to avert their gaze, either literally or metaphorically, through techniques of depersonalisation that enable them to classify their victims as vermin.

As we have just seen, according to the very large numbers of people we have questioned, spiritual awareness awakened either spontaneously or during disciplined meditation returns the experiencer to a level of alertness that makes the obligation to the other person clear. The self-evident nature of such an obligation, once it is aroused, was demonstrated in a remarkable piece of research conducted by Kristen Renwick Monroe, and described in her book *The Heart of Altruism*.[27] Monroe suggests that there is a continuum ranging from self-interest at one pole to altruism at the other pole and that normal human behaviour oscillates

[25] See, *I and Thou*, trans. Ronald Gregor Smith (Edinburgh: T. & T. Clark, 1959).

[26] See *The Levinas Reader*, ed. Sean Hand (Oxford: Blackwell, 1989).

[27] See, *The Heart of Altruism: Perceptions of a Common Humanity* (Princeton University Press, 1996).

between these limits. Her investigation was designed to test whether people's perspective — their way of seeing the world — was reflected in the degree to which they behaved altruistically. She selected four groups of people in the following categories:

- Self made millionaires — representing the rational self-interest end of the spectrum. Such people, if they engaged in apparently altruistic behaviour, would do so in a context where their generosity gained them a sought after personal return, perhaps by financing their political party, university or sports club. Their actions could be most easily explained in terms of current altruism theory in biology,[28] that is, as the result of a calculation that the generous action would trigger a reciprocal act on the part of the institution benefited. For example a wealthy British businessman might hope to be awarded a peerage in the House of Lords in return for a donation to one of the political parties. Or they might come to the aid of their offspring or close relatives because it improved the survival chances of carriers of their 'gene pool'.

- Philanthropists — wealthy people who give away large sums of money to good causes. They may still operate on the basis of self-interest, for example through the gratification they experience when people praise their generosity. Nevertheless they are further along the continuum in the direction of altruism than the millionaires in the first group.

- Heroes — people who have received a reward from the American Carnegie Commission for notably heroic acts that had an element of danger, that is, they had to risk their lives in doing the deed. None of them was a member of a profession where risk taking is part of the job i.e. firemen or soldiers, therefore there was no professional obligation upon them to act heroically. On the other hand they did receive recognition and praise for their heroism.

- People who saved Jews in Nazi-occupied Europe during World War II — in most cases these people could not

---

[28]   There are many books on mainstream altruism theory in biology. One of the most readable is by a journalist, Robert Wright. See *The Moral Animal: Why We Are the Way We Are* (Abacus Books, 1994); also Part I of *The Ant and the Peacock*, written by a professional philosopher and zoologist, Helena Cronin, and published by Cambridge University Press in 1991.

expect any reward for their behaviour. On the contrary they put themselves and their families in danger of imprisonment, torture and death. Their behaviour was thus the most authentically altruistic of all the groups and the most difficult to explain in terms of reciprocal altruism or kin selection. Monroe spoke with ten people in this category who were of course very elderly by the time she met them.

The very detailed narratives Monroe collected from each of the people in the groups convinced her that standard biological explanations of altruism were helpful in understanding the behaviour towards the rational self-interest end of the continuum. They were implausible when it came to accounting for the people who helped Jews to escape the Nazis. Seemingly more traditional explanations did not work either. One of Monroe's interviewees had felt forced to become the mistress of a German officer to buy his silence, after he accidentally discovered that she was protecting a group of Jewish children. The woman was a devout Catholic and disclosed what she was doing when she went to confession, only to be told by the priest to stop her 'immoral behaviour', thereby almost certainly condemning the children to death. She was horrified, left the church and never returned. Monroe comments that something deeper and more primordial than membership of a specific religious organization seems to be operating in cases of this type, that is, the fact that the people protected were recognized as fellow human beings:

> My explanation of altruism, then, centres on this sense of a shared humanity, a perception of self at one with all mankind. It is a much vaguer and subtler concept than the traditional ones – [such as adherence to the codes of a] religion or [the imitation of] role models – that social scientists like to identify. It lacks the comfort of explanatory concepts such as psychic utility or group or kin selection, which are equally intricate but which do not challenge existing orthodoxies based on the norm of self interest. It differs in non-obvious but significant ways from psychological explanations emphasising empathy or perspective taking or extensivity. Yet it was the common factor among all the

altruists I interviewed, the only one that refused to go away under the most careful scrutiny.[29]

My term for what she is describing, is 'relational consciousness'. Monroe's findings when taken with our research on the spiritual life of children enable me to suggest the hypothesis that relational consciousness is the biologically based precursor of both religion and ethics. In other words religions and ethical codes are the socially constructed institutional expressions of that *primordium*. Whilst their common biological source means that they overlap, they are not to be confused with one another. This way of looking at the two great social institutions releases them from being in thrall to each other in ways that are mutually discourteous to both religious believers and agnostics or atheists. The answer to the oft asked question 'Can you have morals without religion? is 'Yes', just as both religious people and atheists can behave immorally. The socially constructed dimensions of either set of beliefs can in principle be detached from primordial relational consciousness.

Some illustrations will help to make clear the way that this affects our understanding of the relationship between morals and religion. The elderly woman describing her disgust with the priest's advice over her affair with the German officer is a good example. The power of her underlying relational consciousness exerted authority over the misjudged application of the socially constructed moral code of the Church in which she had been raised. Her gut ethical sense outranks the mechanical application of a moral rule and though she discarded it there is even a justification within the sacred text of her erstwhile religious community. In the parable of the Good Samaritan, Jesus commends the recognition of common humanity by the despised Samaritan outsider, who stops to help a wounded man. He contrasts it with the dismissal of relational consciousness in favour of maintaining ritual purity by two official representatives of religious orthodoxy.

---

[29]   *Heart of Altruism*, op.cit. p. 206

The social context in which a person comes to maturity is extremely powerful in opening or closing the 'valve' that permits the expression of the underlying predisposition. At times the operation of the valve can be very obvious, the result of a conscious decision based on what the individual takes to be commonsense, that is, the ontological opinions prevailing in the social group to which she belongs. Some years ago a young biology graduate who had been selected at random to participate in a research project on spirituality was describing examples of such experience when she was in her childhood and early teens. When she had finished, I asked her about more recent experiences of that type, to which she replied that she didn't have them any more because when she began studying empirical science she realised that such things are not real, and indeed from that point on, they ceased.

One is reminded of Wordsworth's remarks about the shades of the prison house closing in on his youth. His lines written above Tintern Abbey were composed when he was 28, five years after the actual visit to the Wye valley, in other words they refer to when he was 23 years of age. What he is recalling is the stilling that lies at the heart of contemplative prayer:

> — that serene and blessed mood,
> In which the affections gently lead us on, —
> Until, the breath of this corporeal frame
> And even the motion of our human blood
> Almost suspended, we are laid asleep
> In body, and become a living soul:
> While with an eye made quiet by the power
> Of harmony, and the deep power of joy,
> We see into the life of things.[30]

And for Wordsworth, that life is,

> A presence that disturbs me with the joy
> Of elevated thoughts; a sense sublime
> Of something far more deeply interfused,
> Whose dwelling is the light of setting suns,
> And the round ocean and the living air,

[30] From 'Lines composed a few miles above Tintern Abbey', in, *Wordsworth: The Poems,* ed. John O. Hayden (Harmondsworth: Penguin Books, 1990).

And the blue sky, and in the mind of man;
A motion and a spirit, that impels
All thinking things, all objects of all though
And rolls through all things.[31]

Wordsworth's experience of profundity, of seeing 'into the life of things' is nevertheless vulnerable, as all such experience has become during the course of European history. In the next chapter I want to consider this fragility as someone who, like every other European, has inherited elements of both belief and scepticism as part of our cultural legacy.

---

[31] *Ibid.*

Chapter Two

Cultured Despisers

Men despise religion. They hate it and are afraid it may be true.[1]

I suggested in Chapter One that spirituality, characterised as relational consciousness, is natural to the human species and is the biological precursor of socially constructed systems of religion and ethics. To assert that relational consciousness is biologically inbuilt is to imply that it has evolved through the process of natural selection because it has survival value. Current scientific orthodoxy requires that this refers to the survival of the individual rather than the group. I wish to keep an open mind about that because of Monroe's demonstration of the limited power of conventional theories of kin selection and reciprocal altruism to explain truly selfless behaviour.[2] At any rate the implication of my hypothesis is that the social institutions we call religions have their authentic intuitive origin in this primordial

---

[1] This is the opening sentence of the 17th-century French mathematician Blaise Pascal's *Pensées,* a book of aphorisms compiled as a defence of the Christian religion. See , *Pascal: The Pensées,* trans. J.M. Cohen (Penguin Classics, 1961).

[2] Science has its heretics and in the field of altruism theory the most interesting figures are Elliott Sober and David Sloan Wilson. They base their argument on an updated version of the Aberdeen zoologist V.C. Wynne-Edwards' hypothesis which suggests that the unit of selection in the process of evolution could be the group. Current mainstream opinion disputes the plausibility of Wynne-Edwards' view, which certainly lies at the opposite extreme from Dawkins' notion of the gene as the unit of selection. See, Sober and Wilson's book *Unto Others: The Evolution and Psychology of Unselfish Behavior* (Harvard University Press, 1998); also Wilson's interesting application of his conjecture to the evolution of religion in *Darwin's Cathedral: Evolution, Religion and the Nature of Society* (University of Chicago Press, 2002).

form of awareness. In suggesting this view, I am aware that there are many other explanations of the origin of religion which would require the rejection of such a conjecture, particularly those that see religious beliefs as wrong headed or pathological. Furthermore, if I am right it must surely seem paradoxical to find widespread and increasing rejection of institutional religion as the social expression of what is natural to us, but that is what we do find in large segments of the Western world. In this Chapter I intend to document the undoubted fact of the repudiation of religion in the West. In Chapter Three I will offer an account of the historical and economic processes that have contributed to European secularism, which I interpret as a large-scale culturally constructed error.

Fear and Loathing

Violent dislike of religion can be sampled in generous amounts by anyone who has the temerity to raise the issue in one of the multitude of forums on the Internet concerned with religious belief. I was incautious enough to join one of these groups briefly a couple of years ago, run by the London *Independent* newspaper. Nicknames were assigned to the participants so that all comments were anonymous. As there was so much criticism flying around, I put the question "Why do Europeans find religion so difficult?" The first two replies more or less set the mood for what was to follow. One was from someone whose distaste led them to let me know that they would not waste their valuable time replying to my enquiry, having 'better things to do than to read through the babblings of a religiously impaired person such as yourself'. The other explained to me that religious people are, without exception, infantile and not worth talking to.

In their contempt, both respondents closed down the possibility of measured debate. Moderation in the matter of religion — whether pro or anti — is a scarce commodity, for opinions about it are too near our major value systems to be taken lightly. In these postmodern days it is widely recognized that prejudice in one direction or another is the inevitable accompaniment of all points of view. The very fact that we are brought up situated in a specific cultural background ensures that each of us brings a host of pre-judgements to every controversy in which we participate.[3] True even-handedness in areas that matter to us is an admirable aspiration rather than a real possibility for, as William James said more than a century ago, 'Pretend what we may, the whole man within us is at work when we form our philosophical opinions'.[4] In the circumstances, moderately phrased and honest expression of personal opinion is probably as good as it gets, so what do we find when we investigate reductionist explanations of religion?

Pascal Boyer lies at the mildly reasonable end of the scale and is an important participant in the current controversy. He is an anthropologist who was a scholar in Kings College, Cambridge, but is now based in Washington University in the USA. His assumptions are those of a sceptic, but at the same time he holds the view that religious beliefs can have a biological survival function even when they are entirely without rational or empirical foundation. His studies took him to West Africa where he had a special interest in the religious and metaphysical beliefs of the Fang people who are mainly to be found in Gabon.[5]

One typical example to which he draws our attention is their idea that certain people are born with a small additional internal organ called *evur*, located in the stomach though no one has ever actually seen an *evur*.[6] This is thought to give those who possess the organ special advantages over other people such as having great oratorical skill or business acumen, and also the ability to launch invisible attacks on their competitors. The belief in *evur* is thus func-

---

[3] The book that most clearly demonstrated to me the inevitability of prejudice and therefore the need to be upfront about one's personal stance is Hans-Georg Gadamer's *Truth and Method* published in translation from the German original (Sheed and Ward, 1989).

[4] See, 'Is life worth living?' from William James, *The Will to Believe and Other Essays in Popular Philosophy* (London: Longmans, Green & Co., 1897) (reprinted by Dover Publications, 1956), p. 92

[5] In *Religion Explained: The Human Instincts that Fashion Gods, Spirits and Ancestors* (London: William Heinemann, 2001).

[6] *Ibid.*, p. 76

tional in the tribal understanding of the widespread belief in witchcraft.

Having faith in the *evur* is an example of what Boyer calls a 'counter-intuitive belief', that is to say a belief that contradicts the commonsense categories of reality. He is quick to point out that such beliefs are common to all religions and tells of an occasion when he was dining in Kings College along with some senior theology dons. After he had been describing the beliefs of the Fang he was amused to hear one of the theologians wondering how people could believe such bizarre nonsense, apparently blind to what Boyer saw as the equally strange ideas entertained in Christian theology. In fact, says Boyer, all religions hold to logically bizarre beliefs, including sophisticated world faiths like Christianity and Islam which retain a minimal but real amount of counter-intuitive information. He goes on to discuss a number of traditional Christian beliefs, amongst which he gives prominence to the doctrine of the universality of the divine presence, with the corollary that God can hear our prayers anywhere. According to Boyer, believers implicitly know that this breaches commonsense categories. This, he says, is obvious amongst Roman Catholics, as shown by their habit of praying before statues of saints. Moreover, they even take care to stand within earshot of the statue, and although they know it is made of wood and was manufactured by a woodcarver, they would be outraged if it were to be chopped up.

Though counter-intuitive beliefs are ridiculous as far as Boyer is concerned, they have a vitally important purpose. In a detailed series of arguments supported by reference to practical research, Boyer demonstrates to his own satisfaction the functionality of these beliefs, including faith in the omniscience of God or the Gods. Religious beliefs activate inference systems that 'govern our most intense emotions, shape our interaction with other people, give us moral feelings and organise social groups'.[7] These beliefs have a role in assisting survival and therefore Boyer suggests that the inference systems in question have a structural basis and

---

have evolved through a combination of natural selection and cultural selection (commonly termed Co-Evolution').[8]

In the view of critics of religion, the salient issue is one I mentioned a moment ago, that the spread of counter-intuitive inferences has nothing to do with the truth or falsity of the beliefs, but only with their function in aiding survival. The beliefs in question 'work' because they are based on prior cognitive structures that have already evolved. It helps to make sense of this by considering the analogy of reading. *Homo sapiens* existed for hundreds of thousands of years before writing was invented, but the cognitive skills necessary for reading were in place because they had already evolved for other purposes.[9] Analogously, the cognitive systems involved in the generation of counter-intuitive beliefs were selected for their survival value, not because there is a reality to which religion refers. Cognitive structures that originally evolved for other purposes happen by a happy accident to be useful in this way. Even Boyer can't resist using the language of disease to make the point that

> ... the recurrent properties of religious concepts and norms in different cultures ... are *parasitic upon standard cognitive systems* that evolved outside of religion, such as agency-detection, moral intuition, coalitional psychology and contagion-avoidance. Religious concepts and norms can be explained as a by-product of standard cognitive architecture [my italics].[10]

Another prominent critic of the rationality of religion is Daniel Dennett who is the author of the highly readable

---

[8] See, William Durham's fine book, *CoEvolution: Genes, Culture and Human Destiny* (Stanford University Press, 1991).

[9] Scott Atran holds to a similar view of the evolution of religion in the human species. He, like Dennett, believes that religious beliefs have survival value, but are without ontological importance. See his influential book, *In Gods We Trust: The Evolutionary Landscape of Religion* (New York: Oxford University Press, 2002). For a briefer treatment, see Atran and Norenzayan's interesting paper 'Religion's evolutionary landscape: counterintuition, commitment, compassion, communion', *Behavior and Brain Sciences* 27 (6) (2004), 713–30

[10] From Pascal Boyer's HomePage (10.03.2007). See, <http://artsci.wustl.edu/~pboyer/PBoyerHomeSite/index.html>

Breaking the Spell: Religion as a Natural Phenomenon,[11] which draws to some extent on Boyer's psychological conjectures. Throughout his book Dennett gives the impression of trying to be fair to religious people. His style is friendly and he repeatedly induces a chuckle with witty or dramatic metaphors that add to the reader's enjoyment, but it is his opening image that stays in the mind. If Dennett is anything like most writers he will have given a lot of time to thinking out his opening. I know that I spend more time considering the beginning of a book I am writing than on any other part of the text because the first few sentences set the tone for the whole thing. It is striking therefore that in this even-handed book he begins Chapter One with a description of the behaviour of a parasitic flatworm that is worthy of the horror movie *Alien*.

The lancet fluke *Dicrocelium dendriticum* is a species of flatworm commonly found in pastureland grazed by cattle and sheep. For part of its life cycle the fluke invades the body of an ant and takes control of its nervous system. So-called 'zombie' ants that have become infected undergo a bizarre change in their behaviour. During daylight, instead of avoiding danger, the ants come out into the open and can be seen on blades of grass, repeatedly climbing upwards, struggling towards the sunlight. Why? Because the lancet fluke must find its way inside the stomach of a cow or sheep if it is to move on to the next stage in its life cycle. The worm in the ant's brain forces it to move to a position where there is the greatest probability that a passing animal will swallow it in the process of cropping the grass. The ant has become suicidal, committed to sacrificing its life for the good of the invading parasite. It seems that Dennett wants his readers to carry in their heads from the outset of his book the suspicion that religions are comparable to an appalling infectious disease that takes control of the psyche of its victims.[12]

---

[11] New York: Viking Penguin, 2006.

[12] Dennett's propensity for overtly biased metaphor appears again in his suggestion that atheists should be nicknamed 'Brights', then playing with his opponents after they complain by suggesting that if they like they can

Religion as Evil?

Disease turns up rather frequently as a metaphor in polemics against religion. Another (and as far as I know, independent) suggestion of infection came from the late Sir Francis Crick, Nobel prize winner and co-discoverer of the structure of DNA with James Watson. Crick expressed his distaste for religion by claiming, I assume facetiously, that it was caused by a 'theotoxin' or 'God poison'.[13] The connotation of disease even appears in the title of Aaron Lynch's book *Thought Contagion*,[14] which is on the science of the meme or 'memetics'.

The originator of the term 'meme' is the zoologist Richard Dawkins, Charles Simonyi Professor of the Public Understanding of Science, at Oxford University. In his first book, *The Selfish Gene*[15] published in 1976, Dawkins proposed using the term 'meme' to refer to a unit of cultural transmission analogous to the gene or biological replicator. Memes can be almost any kind of socially transmissible item of culture such as catch phrases, tunes, political slogans, folk beliefs, prejudices and the like. In the case of religious beliefs, which Dawkins thinks are clung on to by the faithful without good reason, he compares them to virus infections.[16]

The major publishing event of 2006, in the midst of what felt like a concerted critical onslaught on religion, was the arrival of Dawkins' tour de force *The God Delusion*.[17] For

---

call themselves 'Supers' after the word 'Supernatural'. Dennett clearly believes in the power of memes as weapons of propaganda, even though they have no relation to his conception of the truth.

[13] Reported in the *Daily Telegraph* on 20 March, 2003.

[14] The full title is *Thought Contagion: How Belief Spreads Through Society* (Basic Books, 1996).

[15] Dawkins, *The Selfish Gene* (Oxford University Press, 1976 and republished in a 30th anniversary edition in 2006).

[16] There is a good discussion of the positive and negative role of memes in survival in William Durham's book *Co-Evolution*. The term 'meme' itself has proved to be very successfully spread through the field of popular science and triggered the publication of numerous books and articles on the subject. Introductions to memetics include Susan Blackmore's *The Meme Machine* (Oxford University Press, 1999), and *Darwinising Culture: the Status of Memetics as a Science*, ed. Robert Aunger (Oxford University Press, 2001).

[17] Dawkins, *The God Delusion* (London, Toronto, Sydney, Auckland and Johannesburg: Bantam Press).

many weeks after it first appeared in the bookshops it remained at or near the top of the best-seller list. As I write it has been nominated as a contender in the Galaxy Awards for Book of the Year, and Dawkins himself has been proposed for the award of author of the year. In part due to his prior eminence as a biological writer and theorist, his religious opinions have obviously struck a chord with the reading public. For that reason alone, his book merits attention.

The design on the cover looks like a bomb going off. It is an appropriate metaphor at more than one level. To find one's deepest convictions the subject of such rage is a sobering experience. At times as I was reading I felt as if I had strayed on to a battlefield with wave after wave of anger breaking over me, for Dawkins has the aggressive certainty of an old fashioned evangelist. His stated aim is that by the time his religiously minded readers have finished the book they will have renounced their foolishness. Those recalcitrant souls who remain unconvinced he dismisses as 'faith heads'[18] and throughout the book he tells many a story about the stupidity, narrow mindedness and bigotry of religious fundamentalists. The apparent reasonableness of more thoughtful religionists also comes under censure for providing sheep's clothing as a cover for the fundamentalist wolves.

Dawkins begins *The God Delusion* with a moving chapter describing his own awe before the marvels of the universe and if this is to count as religion then he pleads guilty. It is

---

[18] There is another side to Dawkins. Earlier this year I arranged to have a chat with him in the Zoology Department in Oxford University. Through a misunderstanding I turned up on the wrong day, but he set aside what he was doing and received me, a stranger, with the greatest courtesy. I was there to gather material for a biography of Alister Hardy, the founder of the Religious Experience Research Unit for which I worked. Hardy would presumably qualify as a 'faith head', having sustained throughout his life a vow made in boyhood to bring about a reconciliation between science and religion. Dawkins told me that he was entirely unaware of Hardy's religious preoccupations when he was a student, though latterly he can hardly have been ignorant of them, for when it was first founded his old professor's Unit was a few hundred yards away from the Zoology Department round the corner in Mansfield Road. He remembered Hardy as a very lovable man, as indeed he was, and in spite of my invitation, declined to offer a comment on his religious opinions.

the introduction of God into the equation that sticks in his craw. In subsequent chapters he demolishes to his own satisfaction Aquinas' proofs of God's existence, Anselm's ontological argument, the argument from personal experience and some lesser defences of faith, then goes on to explain why there is almost certainly no God. The fact that each of these themes has been a battleground of ideas for centuries and has generated libraries full of controversy is no great worry because as far as he can see, the arguments are so ridiculous and so remote from the concrete realities of scientific research that even a schoolboy can see the flaws. Dawkins' own dismissals are accordingly perfunctory, for in his opinion that is all they need to be.[19] For him the clinching evidence comes from Darwin's demonstration of the power of natural selection as the driving force in evolution, thus undermining the argument from design which up to that pivotal moment had been the lynch pin of the believers' arguments.[20]

On the possibility of morals without religion, Dawkins shows convincingly that the moral sense is a human universal, not confined to religious believers. He turns the tables on believers, deploring the savagery of the God of the Old Testament[21] and questioning the morality of central themes

---

[19] There have been many criticisms of *The God Delusion* in the press, which has not prevented it from being an overwhelming publishing success. One of the most amusing reviews was by Terry Eagleton, who compared Dawkins' foray into theology to someone writing an ornithology text on the strength of having read *The Book of British Birds*. See, *London Review of Books* Vol. 28 No. 20, 19 October 2006

[20] Here I think Dawkins is right in seeing the lynch-pin as weak. The Jesuit historian Michael Buckley suggests that at the time of the Renaissance, theologians made a tactical error in abandoning religious experience in favour of basing apologetics on the argument from design. See my comments in Chapter Three and also Buckley's scholarly investigation, *At the Origins of Modern Atheism* (New Haven and London: Yale University Press, 1987); also Buckley's more recent update, *Denying and Disclosing God: the Ambiguous Progress of Modern Atheism* (Yale UP, 2004).

[21] One of the best stories Dawkins tells is borrowed from Evelyn Waugh. In a letter to Nancy Mitford, Waugh gives a hilarious account of an attempt to introduce Winston Churchill's biblically illiterate son Randolph to the Old Testament. Churchill became entranced and kept intruding on other people with thigh slapping and loud chortles of "God, isn't God a shit!" Has Dawkins forgotten that Waugh was himself a committed Catholic and

in the New Testament such as the Atonement. For Dawkins the historical record of religion, its opposition to science, its encouragement of violence in pursuit of its ends, its persecution of out-groups and its alleged indoctrination of children—all these are irrefutable evidence that religion is an evil to be extirpated from the body politic.

There are two unanswered puzzles here. Firstly, it is a sad fact that religions are not the only institutions that can become corrupt. All human organizations without exception are vulnerable to the aberrations Dawkins rightly deplores when they appear in the context of religion. Whether in business, politics, sport or any other collective endeavour, participants fall victim from time to time to the temptations of power. The commonsense response is to correct the aberration and move on, chastened perhaps, but with no thought of abolishing what is self-evidently a vital aspect of the life of the community. Why, in Europe is the case so different when it comes to religion? Secondly, having decided that religion should be got rid of as no more than useless superstition, one is left with the problem of explaining its ubiquity. Being apparently so universal, there is an implication that religious behaviour must have evolved for some purpose. Dawkins turns amongst others to the suggestions by Pascal Boyer that we have already met (as well as Scott Atran who has a rather similar point of view),[22] implying that religious belief evolved almost by error as a by-product of something else. Certainly that could be the case, but why is the more obvious hypothesis discarded, that there really is 'something there'?

Why Now?

The books by Boyer, Dennett, Lynch and Dawkins are only a few out of a spate of recent publications that offer a critical explanation of the religious impulse in the human species. The emergence of a popular, full-blooded and seemingly

---

doesn't he know that there is a discipline that theologians themselves engage in called biblical criticism?

[22]   See, Scott Atran, and Ara Norenzayan, op. cit.

organized hostile critique of religion is relatively new in Britain. It contrasts markedly with the situation in the decade of the 1970s, when religion had an innocent, 'More tea, vicar?' quality. Although the clergy were figures of fun, portrayed in comedy as naïve innocents or fools, they did not merit much in the way of outright anger. Even as late as the 1990s the British prime minister John Major thought he could get away with nostalgic imagery of elderly ladies cycling past the sunlit meadows to early morning communion. In the years following the millennium the atmosphere has changed and the number of books with a negative bias towards religion has accelerated greatly.

Why now? Another title in the genre gives us an important though only partial answer. To a considerable degree these publications are triggered by fear of Islam. Sam Harris' *The End of Faith: Religion, Terror and the Future of Reason*[23] opens, like Dennett's book, with a frightening description of suicidal behaviour, but this time the image presented is of a young Muslim boarding a bus with a bomb under his overcoat, his pockets 'filled with nails, ball bearings and rat poison'. After reading Harris, I turned back to the first page of the preface to *The God Delusion* and noted what I had passed over previously. Dawkins starts his catalogue of disasters attributable to religion with the catastrophic attack on the World Trade Center in New York by Muslim extremists on the fatal day known as '9/11'.[24]

My Muslim friends were as appalled as everyone else by the savagery of the attack. The innocent people killed were of many faiths and included Muslims. Muslim leaders were quick to make public statements pointing to the central emphasis on mercy and peace in the Q'ran, and the violation of that message by the bombers. Nevertheless, it simply is the case that a number of political trouble spots around the world are located in countries with substantial populations of Muslims. The injustices they perceive themselves to have endured are enough to motivate the recruitment of small, highly aggressive radical cells scattered right round

[23] London: Free Press, 2006.
[24] Shorthand for September 11, 2001 the date of the attack.

the Islamic global community (the *umma*). How coherent they are as a political force is not clear, but their potential to launch lethal attacks against targets symbolising the economic and military power of the West is not in doubt after 9/11. Nor, with the acceleration of suicide bomb attacks in Iraq is there any doubt of their ability to foment intra-religious hatred between the Sunni and Shiite branches of Islam.

Most ominously, the alarm caused by the security crisis amounts to the reawakening of a centuries old mistrust, ranging back to folk memories of the Crusades and the expulsion of the Moors from Spain,[25] and symbolised to this day in pubs called the *Saracen's Head* or, in the town where I live, *The Trip to Jerusalem*. Inevitably many of those who fall victim to terrorist attacks are ordinary people who happen to be in the wrong place at the wrong time. The great difficulty of providing an effective defence against this kind of violence has consequently led to increased fearfulness amongst the general population and the introduction of governmental legislation restricting civil liberties. The result is an instinctive backlash against Islam at street level, making everyday life more worrying and precarious for ordinary peaceable Muslims living in the West.

The resurgence of religion. I have remarked on the resurgence of Islam, but this is only part of a more general social change that is not to the liking of secularists. One of the most striking phenomena marking the ending of the 20th century was the unexpected rise of religion to a position of political power on a worldwide scale. The change could not have been forecast on the basis of orthodox secularisation theory as proposed by leading sociologists of religion in the 1950s. This theory holds that religion is a dying force and that as society becomes more rationally ordered the religious institutions will inevitably lose social influence and eventually disappear. In a highly influential book *Religion in Secular*

---

[25] And symbolised by equestrian statues all over Spain, with the title 'Santiago matamoros' ('Saint James the Moorslayer').

Society[26] Bryan Wilson, the head of the Sociology Department in Oxford University drew together the statistical evidence that demonstrated, surely unmistakably, that this was the case.

Current statistics suggest that Wilson's interpretation is still valid for mainstream Christianity in Britain and for a number of other countries in Western Europe. Thus figures for regular church attendance Britain indicate a 20% drop between 1990 and 2000 with rather less than 8% of the adult population involved. This trend if continued forward will, as predicted, witness the virtual disappearance of the Christian institution in the UK by 2050. Sociologists had been beguiled by the situation of religion in Europe into proposing a general law of secularisation applicable to all religion in all places. But as the English sociologist of religion Grace Davie has shown, Europe is a special case. [27]

With hindsight we can see that world events since the Iranian revolution in 1979 were indicating that the classical secularisation hypothesis was flawed and the true state of affairs was much more complex. In his important investigation of *Public Religions in the Modern World*[28] the sociologist José Casanova presented case studies of religious change in four historically Christian countries, illustrating how the religious institutions have entered the arena of public life in a new and politically influential way. Two well-known examples are the role of the Roman Catholic Church in bringing about the collapse of the Communist regime in

---

[26] The late Bryan Wilson was the father figure of secularisation theory in Britain. His book *Religion in Secular Society*, was first published by C.A. Watts in London in 1966. Wilson took an interest in the work of the Religious Experience Research Unit in Oxford, to the extent of being a member of its advisory board. Currently the leading mainstream theorist in the United Kingdom is Steve Bruce, Professor of Sociology at Aberdeen University. Bruce publishes very profusely, so for its provision of striking statistics of institutional decline in Britain, I pick out his controversially titled *God is Dead: Secularisation in the West* (Oxford: Blackwell, 2002).

[27] See, *Europe the Exceptional Case: Parameters of Faith in the Modern World*, op. cit. Chapter 1.

[28] Published in 1994 by the University of Chicago Press. Casanova gives a convincing account of the subtleties of the changing situation in the Christian churches.

Poland, and the rise of the Christian Right as a political force in the United States.

The increased political power of Christian Fundamentalism in America is certainly an extraordinary spectacle, alarming not only to secularist critics but to many thoughtful Christians who are disturbed by its hostility to aspects of science that conflict with a literal reading of the Bible. The complexity of the picture is further demonstrated by sharp contrasts in secularisation in countries adjacent to each other. Thus, the Hungarian sociologist of religion Miklos Tomka notes how in the 1999 European Values Study, Poland had the highest percentage of people declaring themselves as religious at 93.9% whilst the former East Germany, which shares a border with Poland, had the lowest at 29.4%.[29]

The special character of European secularism. Neither the rise of Islam to renewed political power, nor the reawakening of ancient religious hostilities adequately accounts for the nature of the secularism that is peculiar to European culture. Its origins lie much further back in history, though how far back is a disputed question. On the basis of his anthropological studies the French sociologist Émile Durkheim claimed that 'In the beginning all is religious'[30] with atheism appearing relatively late in human history. There are some references that seem to connote unbelief in the literature of classical Greece. One of the doyens of 19th century atheism, Karl Marx, placed a quote from Aeschylus — 'I hate the pack of gods' — in the preface to the doctoral thesis he presented to the University of Jena in 1841. Of course if taken literally, hatred of the gods implies that they are there to be hated. Similar uncertainties surround other figures from the classical period claimed by modern atheists as their forerunners, including Democritus, who first

[29] See *Religion and Social Change in Post-Communist Europe*, ed. , Borowik and Tomka (Krakow: Zaklad Wydawniczy »NOMOS«, 2001), especially Miklos Tomka's article on 'Religious change in East-central Europe', pp. 11–27

[30] In the *Revue Philosophique*, Vol. 44, pp. 646–51, commenting on Antonio Labriola's *Essays on the Materialist Conception of History*.

taught the atomic theory of matter, Anaxagoras who it is said was expelled from Athens for his atheism and the materialist philosopher Epicurus. Epicurus is sometimes claimed as the originator of the well-known argument for atheism based on the existence of evil: 'Is God willing to prevent evil, but not able? Then he is not omnipotent. Is he able, but not willing? then he is malevolent. Is he both able and willing? Then whence comes evil? Is he neither able nor willing? Then why call him God?'

However, in his authoritative review of atheism in antiquity, Jan Bremmer[31] comes to the conclusion that it was never held by more than a very small minority of people in that period. Bremmer adds that the same situation prevailed in Europe throughout mediaeval times. Christian culture embraced the whole of life to such an extent that atheist ideas seemed implausibly remote from reality. By the 17th century rumours of widespread disbelief became commonplace for the first time although it is impossible to be sure of their accuracy. That this process was certainly under way is indicated by Pascal's well known observation that, 'Men despise religion. They hate it and are afraid it may be true'. In *A History Of Atheism In Britain: From Hobbes To Russell*, [32]David Berman comments on the nebulousness of the data on the numbers of atheists in the country during that period and adds that the jumpiness of churchmen made them deny the possibility of atheism, at the same time as writing increasing numbers of pamphlets warning of its dangers. Even the celebrated unbelief of Thomas Hobbes, (who is the Hobbes in Berman's title) is questioned by A.P. Martinich, a respected student of the period. Martinich judges that he was an orthodox Calvinist in his views,[33] and Certainly Hobbes' low opinion of human beings in the state of nature is not out of keeping with Calvin's dictum that we are all 'children of wrath'.

---

[31]   See Jan M Bremmer, 'Atheism in antiquity', in *The Cambridge Companion to Atheism*, ed. Michael Martin (Cambridge University Press, 2007), pp. 11–26.

[32]   London: Croom Helm, 1988.

[33]   See Martinich's book, *Hobbes* (London: Routledge, 2005), Chapter 6.

The horror with which atheism was commonly viewed continues to complicate historical judgement even as late as the latter part of the 18th century, in the case of David Hume. His atheism seems transparent, for in the *Dialogues Concerning Natural Religion*, published in 1779, the most convincing arguments are those that strip the concept of God of religious meaning. Yet in the *Dialogues* he also denies his unbelief when he writes: 'I next turn to the atheist, who, I assert, is only nominally so, and can never possibly be in earnest.'[34] Berman also reminds us of a second denial by Hume when he dined with the famous French encyclopaedist, Baron d'Holbach. Holbach's fellow encyclopaedist Denis Diderot gave a description of the occasion:

> The first time that M. Hume found himself at the table of the Baron he was seated beside him. I do not know for what purpose the English[35] (*sic*) philosopher took it into his head to remark to the Baron that he did not believe in atheists, that he had never seen any. The Baron said to him: 'Count how many we are here.' We are eighteen. The Baron added: 'It is not too bad a showing to be able to point out to you fifteen at once; the three others have not made up their minds'.[36]

I have said as much as is necessary to suggest the nature of the equivocations over the admission of atheism that lasted well into the 19th century in Europe, and in certain parts of the Western world still have force.[37] It was also during the

---

[34] Hume, *Dialogues Concerning Natural Religion*, ed. Norman Kemp Smith (Oxford University Press, 1935), p. 268.

[35] Hume was of course a Scotsman.

[36] Quoted in Berman, op.cit. p. 101

[37] As a child brought up in a strongly religious community in the North of Scotland, my own associations with the word were deeply negative; atheism was something from which one shrank back in horror. It was the final legacy of a history that initially threatened professed atheists with imprisonment or death, through to the 19th century when amelioration meant that atheists' lives were spared, but they were in danger of losing their means of livelihood. In certain parts of the Western world the latter danger still remains, though often at an informal level, for example in the 'Bible belt' in the United States. Of course in states that are or were officially atheist, as in the case of the former Soviet Union, the situation was reversed and it was believers who had to fear for their safety. The strange nightmare world of Stalinist suppression is evoked with great power in Mikhail

first half of the 19th century that a highly sophisticated account of the alleged source of religious belief, seen as a universal error, was put forward by Ludwig Feuerbach, and subsequently modified by numerous critics including Karl Marx, Sigmund Freud, and Emile Durkheim.[38] These names are amongst the major icons of the modern intellectual tradition and underpin the mainstream account of religion offered in most Western academic institutions up to our own day.

Secular and religious atheism. Sceptical orthodoxy places Hume at a pivotal point in this critique of religious belief. From then on, or so it is claimed, religious discourse was finally and indisputably shown up as supernaturalist claptrap. The criticism of religion that comes from secularist sources is thus utterly radical. No reform can ever be good enough because religion is flawed in its most basic axiom, that there is a transcendent dimension of our human experience that is *sui generis*. For the sceptic the positing of such a dimension is at best an infantile error, at worst evidence of mental illness. Hence by definition religious institutions that make such claims are guilty of purveying falsehoods that divert people from their best interests. For that reason alone, religion is a danger to society and must be attacked in the way that Dawkins and others advocate.

At this point it is important to stress that the issue is made complex by a fact that we have already adverted to, the atheism characteristic of several major religious groups in Asia, including Hindu followers of the Vedanta, the Southern Buddhists and the Jains. These communities are either agnostic about God or deny God's existence. They sound as

Bulgakov's novel *The Master and Margarita*, available in several editions, for example in Penguin Modern Classics (2004).

[38] There is debate about Durkheim. Alister Hardy believed a careful reading of his master-work on religion, *The Elementary Forms of the Religious Life* would show that Durkheim was not a reductionist at least in relation to religious experience. On the other hand most followers of Durkheim take it that when he referred to religious experience as 'effervescence' he implicitly prefaced the word with 'nothing but'. For Hardy's views, see his second set of Gifford Lectures in Aberdeen University, published as *The Divine Flame*, Lecture III, (Collins, 1966), pp. 56–80.

if they ought to be making common cause with European secularism, but Westerners need to beware of equating them. In fact they differ significantly in the fact that they do not deny the reality of transcendence. They are participants in an ongoing debate about transcendence that is internal to religion.

As I mentioned on an earlier page, when we look more closely at the praxis of the great religions it is obvious that there is ambivalence about the experience of transcendence; whether it is the discovery of absolutely impersonal monism, or on the other hand a deeply personal encounter with God. Judging by what practitioners say of their experience in both theistic and atheistic religious traditions such experience simply is ambivalent. In Christianity the ambivalence is represented by the *apophatic* tradition, which teaches that no human language is adequate to refer to God, so it is more appropriate either to use language to make negative statements about what God is not, or to remain silent. It may be significant that this approach to transcendence is particularly appealing to people who have advanced some way in the life of prayer and are thus, so to speak, drawing upon the results of a practical investigation. Although Theravadin or Southern Buddhism is commonly described as atheist, ambivalence rather than any absolute statement is also characteristic of Buddhist reflections on transcendence and this is expressed in the well known Buddhist *trilemma*: Everything is either true, or not true, or both true and not true, or neither true nor not true; that is the Buddha's teaching.

Concluding Comment

When Samuel Preus' text *Explaining Religion: Criticism and Theory from Bodin to Freud*[39] came out in 1987 it was recommended to me by a sociologist friend as a clear account of the historical progress of attempts at explaining the phenomenon of religion in secular terms. I take it that Preus sees it as the story of humanity's long journey of emancipa-

---

[39]   Published by Yale University Press in Newhaven and London in 1987.

tion from the shackles of superstition. It occurred to me as I was thinking about what he says, that another way of reading Preus would be to interpret his narrative as a deconstruction of the processes that led to the ignoring and repression of an essential aspect of our humanity.

Critics of religion see the default position of the human being as atheism. We are born as little atheists and in the process of being socialised we acquire a set of religious beliefs. I say the evidence points in almost exactly the opposite direction. In what historically is the normal situation, we are born with a vivid awareness of a transcendent dimension to our experience and we learn how to interpret it via the local religious culture, thus integrating it into the pattern of our lives. It is evident that social construction plays a pivotal part here, with the expectation of the theist and the atheist opening and closing awareness of different aspects of transcendence. In the case of socialisation into the European sceptical tradition the whole universe of discourse is closed down. We learn to blot it out and we become secular atheists. How this came about is the subject of the next chapter.

Chapter Three

The Lonely European

Away … with every concern that is not altogether my concern! You think that at least the 'good cause' must be my
concern? What's good? What's bad? Why I myself am my
concern, and I am neither good nor bad. Neither has meaning for me. The divine is God's concern: the human, man's.
My concern is neither the divine nor the human, not the
true, good, just, free etc, but is — unique, as I am unique.
Nothing is more to me than myself![1]

On the penultimate day of December 1902 in a convent in
Plaistow, North London, a woman known locally as Mary
Smith died at the age of 84. She had lived there in devout
obscurity apart from some minor missionary activity in the
surrounding streets, urging passers by to read the Bible and
distributing uplifting tracts to those who would have them.
The nuns arranged for her body to be laid to rest not far
away in St Patrick's Catholic cemetery in Leytonstone
where, although she has no headstone, the site of her grave
can still be identified today.[2]

A dull conclusion to a dull life, you may think, but the
anonymity of Mary's ending conceals a dramatically different story in her youth. Her baptismal name was Marie
Dahnhardt. She was born in 1818 and brought up in a small
town near Lübeck in North Germany. In her twenties she
spurned provincial life in favour of the excitements of
Berlin where she became a member of a group of political
dissidents at one time associated with Karl Marx and calling

---

[1]   See, Max Stirner, *The Ego and Its Own*, trans. Steven Byington (London:
      Rebel Press, 1993), p. 5
[2]   My thanks are due to John Sears for identifying the spot in Leytonstone
      cemetery where Mary is buried (Plot F6, Grave 94).

themselves 'the Free Ones' (*Die Freien*).[3] They were to be found most days in Hippel's Weinstube, a drinking establishment where Marie was remembered as a glamorously eccentric cigar and pipe-smoking blonde. She drank beer, tankard for tankard with the men, revelled in scurrilous gossip and in a way could be considered an emancipated feminist before her time. She also got married in a ridiculously lampooning version of the legally required religious ceremony to the strangest and most controversial member of the group, Johann Caspar Schmidt.

There is no record of quite why Marie's life story followed its extraordinary pattern or how she came to end her days in an English convent. In choosing to marry Schmidt she had linked herself to a man who wrote what is arguably the most extreme statement of philosophical individualism ever to appear in print. In the rest of this chapter I want to outline the story of the development of European atheism as the inevitable outcome of individualism, of which Schmidt was such a remarkable representative. In the process of unfolding that narrative I hope that its impact upon the religious tradition of the West will become clear, along with an intuition as to the reason for Marie's decision to return to that tradition.

Egotism as a Way of Life

Marie's husband Johann was better known by his nickname, 'Max Stirner', or 'the highbrow', so called because of his very high forehead [German: *stirn*]. There is no photographic record of Max's appearance, but on one occasion Friedrich Engels paid the group a visit, during which he made a rough sketch of the members. They look as if they are in the midst of a drunken argument, arms waving and a chair kicked over. Stirner is standing apart from the boister-

[3]   *Die Freien* were a small group made up former members of Bruno Bauer's 'Doktorklub' to which Marx had belonged, though Marx had left Berlin before Marie arrived, possibly at the end of 1841, so the two never met.

ous action, smoking a cigarette and looking very much an outsider. Engels wrote a comic poem about him:[4]

> Look at Stirner, look at him, the peaceful enemy of all constraint
> For the moment, he is still drinking beer,
> Soon he will be drinking blood as though it were water.
> When others cry savagely 'down with the kings'
> Stirner immediately supplements 'down with the laws also'.
> Stirner full of dignity proclaims; you bend your will power
> and you dare to call yourselves free,
> You become accustomed to slavery;
> Down with dogmatism; down with law.[5]

Other contemporary accounts depict Stirner as a passionless isolate with no true friends. This is consistent with one description of him as having 'a quiet inclination to ridicule' and with a remark overheard on another occasion that he felt he was in a madhouse surrounded by fools. Physical intimacy was probably difficult for him. At the time when he persuaded Marie to become his wife he had already been married. He told someone that he had once observed his previous partner unconsciously exposing herself in bed whilst fast asleep and the sight so disturbed him that from then on he could hardly bear to touch her.

This odd and lonely man was also a proponent of extreme atheism. Like the other members of *Die Freien*, he was a neo-Hegelian, that is, a radical follower of the Berlin philosopher G.W.F. Hegel. The term 'neo-Hegelian' is in a way a misnomer and needs a little unpacking. Though Stirner went along with Hegel in the sense that he was impressed by his dialectical method of philosophising, he, like other members of the group was utterly opposed to Hegel's idealism as expressed in the belief that physical reality is the unfolding of an idea in the mind of the Absolute. In popular terms this was often put as, 'man is an idea in the mind of God'.

It was a fellow member of *Die Freien*, Ludwig Feuerbach, who famously inverted Hegel's philosophy, asserting that

[4] The only other surviving picture of Stirner is a portrait sketch drawn from memory by Engels in 1892.
[5] Quoted in 'Stirner and Marx' by Alexander Green, in *non serviam* #23, April 2006, p. 2 [Available on the Internet at http://www.nonserviam.com/magazine/issues/23.html]

'God is an idea in the mind of man'. Feuerbach's first major book on the subject, *The Essence of Christianity*, was published in 1841[6] and it was here that he introduced the notion of religion as 'projection'. He suggested that when theologians write about the attributes of God, they are in reality projecting all that is best and admirable in the human species, or the 'essence' of humanity, onto a mythical figure in the heavens. That is to say, if you want to know the truth about human beings it is to be found under the appearances of theology. For Feuerbach the Christian religion is a kind of concealed anthropology and the task facing humankind, if it is to become emancipated, is the dismissal of the imaginary father figure in the sky and the re-appropriation of the high and noble purposes that belong to our 'species being'.

For a short time after the appearance of *The Essence of Christianity* Feuerbach was hailed as a genius, but his reputation was to suffer twin blows in 1845, with the publication of Marx's eleven *Theses on Feuerbach* and Max Stirner's only book, *The Ego and its Own* (incidentally dedicated 'to my sweetheart Marie Dahnhardt').[7] The brief *Theses on Feuerbach* is much the better known of the two works but as scholarly research is now revealing, Stirner's critique is ultimately the more damaging.[8] He of course agreed that religious belief was the result of a projection, but pointed out in his book that Feuerbach had failed to follow out the logical consequences of his argument to the limit. If believers in God are putting themselves in thrall to a myth of their own invention, then exactly the same can be said of all other situations where individuals put themselves under obligation to some external ideal. So, love of one's country, self-sacrifice for the sake of others, seeking to abide by a moral code, taking up a cause because of a belief in honour or jus-

---

[6]   Translated into English by George Eliot and produced in numerous editions, for example my copy was published in 1989 by Prometheus Books, Amherst, New York.

[7]   *The Ego and its Own*, Op. cit.

[8]   The argument is clearly summarised in an article by Frederick M. Gordon 'The debate between Feuerbach and Stirner: an introduction', in *The Philosophical Forum*, 8, 2–3–4, (1976). [Reproduced on the Internet at http://www.nonserviam.com/stirner/reviews/gordon.html]

tice — these have precisely the same status as religious belief. Feuerbach's idealism is simply a concealed form of religion, placing oneself under the power of a gaggle of myths without substance.

The only concrete reality, says Stirner, is myself — and all my actions, if they are rational, are governed by selfishness. Self-seeking is not a vice for there are no such things as good and evil, only that which does or does not contribute to my own wellbeing:

> The fear of God in the proper sense was shaken long ago, and a more or less conscious "atheism," externally recognizable by a widespread "unchurchliness," has involuntarily become the mode. But what was taken from God has been superadded to Man, and the power of humanity grew greater in just the degree that of piety lost weight: "Man" is the God of today, and fear of Man has taken the place of the old fear of God. *But, because Man represents only another Supreme Being, nothing in fact has taken place but a metamorphosis in the Supreme Being, and the fear of Man is merely an altered form of the fear of God. Our atheists are pious people.* [italics added][9]

Against such piety Stirner engages in extravagant rhetoric on behalf of the Ego. All relationships are power struggles[10] and a matter of mutual exploitation, even from birth:

> From the moment when he catches sight of the light of the world a man seeks to find out himself and get hold of himself out of its confusion, in which he with everything else gets tossed about in motley mixture. But everything that comes in contact with the child defends itself in turn against his attacks, and asserts his own persistence. Accordingly because each thing cares for itself and at the same time comes into constant collision with other things, the combat of self-assertion is unavoidable. Victory or defeat — between the two alternatives the fate of the combat wavers. The victor becomes the lord, the vanquished one the subject ... but both remain enemies, and always lie in wait: they watch for each other's weaknesses — children for those of their parents and parents for those of their children

---

[9] Stirner, op. cit. p. 241
[10] Could this be construed as an anticipation of the ideas of Michel Foucault, I wonder?

(their fear for example); either the stick conquers the man,
or the man conquers the stick.[11]

Stirner's self-centredness comes perilously near to solip-
sism, for he feels free to manipulate any situation without
regard to any consideration outside himself. And in the
pursuit of advantage, all tactics are legitimate, lying, steal-
ing, even physical violence and murder. In his intense
espousal of egotism[12] Stirner represents the startling and
unsettling endpoint of a social process that is unique to
European culture, the construction of modern individualism. Where had such extreme individualism come from and
how did it impinge on Marie Dahnhardt?

Of course there is nothing new about looking after Number One. There have always been plenty of people who
focus on their personal needs to the exclusion of others. Historical records are full of accounts of brutality in pursuit of
personal gain, as is the Bible, especially in the pages of the
Old Testament. Nevertheless our ancestors were in no
doubt that avarice was wrong. In mediaeval Europe it was
considered one of the most disgusting sins punishable,
according to Dante, by consignment to the fourth level of
Hell. But it is also in Europe that a vigorous advocacy of
self-interest took shape with such force that it has come to
pervade social life in a way that is distinctive to the Western
world. When I use the term 'Western' I have in mind the
continent of Europe and those parts of the world to which
Europeans have either migrated or strongly influenced the
way of life of the indigenous peoples. I am therefore considering a phenomenon of global proportions. Furthermore,
since individualism or self-interest is by definition at log-
gerheads with the relational consciousness discussed in the
previous chapter, its damaging influence on people's spiritual lives has also been on a very large scale. In the remain-
der of this chapter I shall attempt in a preliminary fashion to
identify some of the social processes that have brought

---

[11] *Ibid.*, p. 9
[12] For an interesting philosophical discussion of Stirner's egotism, see John P.
Clark, *Max Stirner's Egotism* (London: Freedom Press, 1976).

about this spiritual destruction, of which Stirner's anarchism is an extreme symptom.

The Precursors of Individualism

That a major shift of consciousness took place in Europe between the Sixteenth and Eighteenth centuries is not in doubt. This can be demonstrated by examining the popular literature of the period. In his masterly study, *Myths of Modern Individualism*[13] the literary historian Ian Watt examines four major narratives or folk myths that are deeply embedded in the awareness of Europeans and which reflect changing public attitudes to individualism. The stories of *Faust*, *Don Quixote* and *Don Juan* mirror an earlier, critical view of people who stand out from the group and do things differently. They come to no good, as illustrated by the fate of Faust and Don Juan who are cast into hell, whilst Don Quixote is the great laughing stock of European literature. By 1719, the year that Daniel Defoe published *Robinson Crusoe*, the status of the individual has begun to be much more positive, for Crusoe is neither a villain nor is he mocked. The story of his self-sufficiency has grown into one of the best known of all fictional narratives and whilst we grin at his occasional naivety, his status is not far from being heroic.

Students of European history have identified a sequence of political and economic influences underlying this change in the standing of the individual. To these I shall turn in a moment, but first it is necessary to identify two precursors of those events, stages of development gone through by all literate human beings regardless of their cultural background: these are, the acquiring of language and learning to read and write. Between them these achievements play a major role in establishing people's recognition of themselves as individuals.

Acquiring language. Since nobody from the modern scientific community was around to overhear it, the question of when

[13] *Myths of Modern Individualism: Faust, Don Quixote, Don Juan, Robinson Crusoe* (Cambridge University Press, 1996).

human beings first began to talk is not answerable with certainty. If we make a timid guess and suppose that language is limited to our own species, *Homo sapiens*, it has been around for perhaps 200,000 years. It may have been installed for much longer. There are ways of making an informed estimate based on knowledge of the functions of certain anatomical regions of the brain. Although brain tissue is too soft to leave a relic, the form of the inside of a fossil skull can give information about the shape and size of the adjacent surfaces of the brain. These include *Broca's area* in the frontal lobe of the left cerebral hemisphere and *Wernicke's area* in the left temporal lobe, both of which are known to be concerned with the ability to speak. On that basis, a study of the skulls of members of a quite separate and much older human species found in East Africa, *Homo habilis*, suggests that they might have had linguistic ability. If that is a reasonable deduction, it would take the point at which language evolved back to two million years ago or more.[14]

Either way the important point to recognise is that the parts of the brain concerned with language acquisition appeared a very long time ago and with them the ability to recognise oneself as distinct from the rest of reality. Young children typically begin speaking at around eighteen months, and research studies indicate a contrast between the self-awareness that is possible before and after that point. Newborn children operate in ways that implicitly recognize a distinction between self and other, as has been demonstrated in the remarkable work of the Hungarian psychologist Emese Nagy on infant intersubjectivity.[15] The baby is inherently aware that 'I know' but is unable to reflect on the fact. With the coming of language and in particular

[14] For further information on these questions see the articles by Terrence Deacon on 'Biological aspects of language' (pp. 128–33) and C.B. Stringer on 'Evolution of early humans' (pp. 241–51) in *The Cambridge Encyclopedia of Human Evolution*, ed. Steve Jones, Robert Martin and David Pilbeam (Cambridge University Press, 1994).

[15] Nagy, E. & Molnar, P. (2004). 'Homo imitans or Homo provocans? Human imprinting model of neonatal imitation'. *Infant Behavior and Development*, 27: 54–63.

the ability to use personal pronouns the infant is able to articulate the insight 'I know that I know' and hence discriminate verbally between subject and object.

Language also gives a framework that enables the child to employ recollection and imagination reflectively. Once we can attach a name to the objects around us they can, so to speak, step forward in our minds in contrast to their surroundings. Through the use of memory they can be made central to our awareness at other times and in other places when they are not directly present.[16] The object that above all others is constantly drawn attention to by admiring parents is the baby itself, who at the same time is learning to use personal pronouns like 'You', 'Me' and 'I'. As the awareness of 'I' increasingly becomes available it can be thought about in the same way as any other object of consciousness. 'I' begin to accumulate a personal narrative that makes up my unique life history or individuality.

Finally, it is important not to lose sight of the fact that the process of individualisation is a social phenomenon, proceeding in the company of others. This is highlighted by studies of the way that the form of social products like specific languages or detailed etiquette in different cultures makes for subtle differences in self-understanding. One example that is relevant to the present discussion is the way that the grammar of Indo-European languages uses the first person to indicate that whoever is speaking is morally responsible for what they say. By contrast the use of the first person in Japanese usually has reference to the 'me-group' to which the person belongs, rather than to the specific individual making the utterance. Thus already in the way language is used, the sense of oneself as a separate individual is more strongly marked in European than in Japanese experience.[17]

---

[16] For a popular discussion of the effect of language on self awareness, see John McCrone *The Ape that Spoke: Language and the Evolution of the Human Mind* (London: Picador, 1990).

[17] The example is taken from Peter Muhlhausler and Rom Harré, *Pronouns and People* (Oxford: Blackwell, 1990), p. 112

Learning to read and write The next step in acquiring detachment from one's surroundings happens when we learn to read and write. These skills may seem natural because most people in literate societies pick them up when they are very young. They are in fact very recent novelties when compared with the lengthy prehistory of language acquisition. This is vividly brought home in the late Walter Ong's fine book *Orality and Literacy*,[18]

> language is so overwhelmingly oral that of all the many thousands of languages — possibly tens of thousands — spoken in the course of human history only around 106 have ever been committed to writing to a degree sufficient to have produced literature, and most have never been written at all. Of the some 3000 languages spoken that exist today, only some 78 have a literature.[19]

In the case of people who use those languages that do possess an extensive literature, facility in reading and writing was relatively rare until a few generations ago. Only during the past 150 years in most Western nations has there been an organized attempt to ensure that everyone is literate, a skill made necessary by the rapidly increasing complexity of life associated with the industrial revolution. Even today a significant minority of the population fails to master the difficult art of reading, reminding us that learning to read is an artificial accomplishment, different in kind from a primordial skill like learning to speak. It follows that for many millennia human consciousness was evolving in response to the selection pressures of an environment that was remote from the need to interpret the complex symbol systems that go to make up a written text. The *normal* mode in which our consciousness operates is one that is innocent of the skills of reading and writing.

What happens to our natural awareness when we move into the abnormal world of the printed page, or even more

---

[18]   Walter J Ong SJ, *Orality and Literacy: the Technologizing of the Word* (London and New York: Routledge, 1982).

[19]   Op. cit. p. 7

remotely, onto the Internet?[20] Trying to imagine ourselves back into a time when we were unable to read is unlikely to succeed, for as Ong explains,

> Graphocentrism is hard to escape, since we have been shaped by writing. The fact that we do not commonly feel the influence of writing on our thoughts shows that we have interiorized the technology of writing so deeply that without tremendous effort we cannot separate it from ourselves or even recognize its presence and influence'.[21]

An alternative strategy of investigation is to observe what life is like for our contemporary fellow adults who have never been able to read. A most remarkable pioneering attempt to do this was initiated in the 1930s in the remote hill country on either side of the border between Uzbekistan and Kyrgyzstan in the former Soviet Union. Although the people living there are Muslim and thus dependent on knowing the contents of the Q'ran for their belief system, they were at that time members of a primary oral culture, meaning that the general community had never been literate. At the beginning of the 1930s all that was about to change, for it was then that Stalin decreed that everyone throughout the USSR must be taught to read. Collective farms were being set up across the Union and literacy was a *sine qua non* if the peasants were to come to grips with the complexities of running such large scale establishments.

At the time, Alexander Luria was a young psychologist in the University of Moscow and he took the opportunity to make a comparative study of the ways people handled intellectual tasks before and after learning to read and write.[22] Luria's major finding from his fieldwork was that

---

[20] One only has to think of the way that reading and writing dominate our everyday lives, now added to by the ubiquity of the Internet and the World Wide Web, to begin to see that the mode of action of our consciousness is very different from that of our non-literate forebears. See, for example, John L. Locke, *Why we Don't Talk to Each Other any More: The Devoicing of Society* (New York: Simon & Schuster, 1998).

[21] Ong, op. cit. p. 24

[22] See Luria, *Cognitive Development: Its Cultural and Social Foundations.* trans. Martin Lopez-Morillas and Lynn Solotaroff; ed. Michael Cole (Harvard University Press, 1976). It is a striking commentary on the Stalinist censorship of scientific findings that were potentially discordant with the

intellectual tasks that are elementary for literate people can be surprisingly difficult for people who are unable to read or write. One vivid illustration comes from his experiments on the ability to undertake abstract classification. The peasant women in the region were well known for their subtle colour sense as displayed in their embroidery. Yet when Luria invited them to classify the colours of the skeins of wool they used in their work in terms of category—shades of blue, red, yellow and so on—they were frequently baffled. Instead of grouping them abstractly they made comparisons based on their immediate concrete experience, for example saying that one skein of wool looked like 'pig's dung', whereas another similarly coloured skein looked like 'rotten teeth'. On the other hand, semi-educated and only recently literate collective farm workers were easily able to classify the colours. Luria asked illiterate men to do a similar kind of classification, and like the women they found it difficult to stand back intellectually from the immediate practicalities of what they were doing. For example woodcutters might classify saws, axes, hammers and logs together, but not saws, axes, hammers and shovels. The abstract category of 'tools' did not make immediate sense, whereas the concrete 'things involved in working with wood' was more meaningful.

Luria's insight was to realise that these responses were not due to lack of intelligence, but were imposed on the structure of thought by the dependence of members of illiterate societies on communal memory. Walter Ong has summarised the cognitive differences between illiterate and literate people detected by Luria and subsequently by other researchers working in primary oral cultures. Two points are relevant to my argument:

- Abstract thinking is difficult for members of oral cultures because it requires them to stand back from the immedi-

political objectives of the regime, that public access to Luria's work was not available for more than 30 years after it had been completed. This is discussed by Michael Cole in his epilogue to Luria's autobiography. See *The Autobiography of Alexander Luria: A Dialogue with the Making of a Mind* (Mahwah, NJ: Lawrence Erlbaum Associates, 2006), pp. 213-7

ate concrete situation. The problem about stepping away from immediacy is that it reduces the vividness of the here-and-now reality and gets in the way of the primary need to remember, for apart from memory there is no other way for illiterate people to store knowledge. Living memories are the fragile repositories of information that will be replaced in literate societies by libraries, filing cabinets and back-up copies. In primary oral societies the collective memory of the whole community performs the role of a library, in the sense that information is gathered by consulting other people's memories rather than books.

- It follows that people belonging to oral cultures are likely to be much more communally minded than literate groups. There is also a good reason for such communities to be deeply conservative, because doing something new risks losing vital traditional knowledge through forgetfulness.

In contrast to this necessary conservatism, literacy continues the process of individualisation initiated by the ability to speak, but with much greater impact. Literacy drastically reduces the need to remember everything, since information can be stored in written form, whilst reading gives us the ability to move in our imagination out of the concrete here-and-now in any direction a book can take us. Also, the fact that we gain information from words on a page encourages the idea that knowledge is something independent of us that we can examine in a detached way. Most strikingly, literacy throws open the door to a private world, not dependent on directly shared memory but on the limitations of one's library.

The complexities of modern society are so great that we would be unable to manage them without the skills of literacy and this is compounded hugely and in contradictory and as yet unpredictable ways by the revolution in electronic communication. The two aspects of our experience that very often get overlooked in the process are (a) the rich, concrete immediacy of our relationship with the here-and-now and (b) our immediate sense of belonging to and being continuous with the surrounding community.

We have seen in the previous chapter that the locus of communication with sacred reality is pre-eminently in this same holistic awareness of immediacy. Thus, if people are to maintain contact with the spiritual dimension when they become literate they need to have some system for protecting immediate awareness. As 'people of the Book' the traditional faith communities of Jews, Christians and Muslims of course respect literacy highly. But at the same time as beginners are learning to read and write, the greatest care is taken to give instruction in how to stay in touch with their spiritual lives via the skills of contemplative prayer or meditation. In monotheistic religions this requires the regular practice of raising the heart and mind to God in the here-and-now, or what the Jesuit Jean-Pierre de Caussade[23] calls attending to the 'sacrament of the present moment'. In those religions that decline to comment on the existence of God there are closely parallel practices. As we saw previously, in Theravada Buddhism *vipassana* or awareness meditation requires a similar focusing on the here-and-now, assisted by attention to the act of breathing whilst sitting, or observing the fine detail of the movements of the feet in walking meditation.[24]

For the committed member of a religious community these practices are not undertaken casually. They are timetabled into a structured routine, in many cases repeated several times each day. In every case, ranging

[23] See, *Self Abandonment to Divine Providence* (London: Collins/Fontana, 1971).

[24] See, Nyanaponika Thera, *The Heart of Buddhist Meditation* (Newburyport, MA: Red Wheel/Weiser, 1976). The formal practice of shifting one's attention to immediacy produces an awareness of a potentially immense profusion of sensory phenomena, bodily feelings, anxieties, fantasies that are the subject matter of meditative exercises like *vipassana*. Some years ago I was involved in a project designed to help pupils in secondary school to investigate the here and now of their awareness. The feedback from teachers and pupils in the schools where the methodology was being tested was remarkable. The great majority of the students had never taken part in even the simplest of meditative exercises, for example choosing to be aware of the sounds in the classroom, or attending to their breathing for a period of one or two minutes at most. Frequently they were astonished and fascinated by their enriched awareness, previously obscured by the commitment to the line mode produced by their education.

from Vespers to *vipassana*, the ultimate purpose is to culti-
vate a state of steady alertness to here-and-now reality, or to
put it in the Christian terms of St Paul, to pray without ceasing. One can see something of what this means, even in the
secularised West, in areas where there are substantial numbers of first or second generation Muslim immigrants. Compared to most members of the indigenous population they
are much less caught into the assumptions of the Enlighten-
ment critique of religion and therefore not so prone to edgy
defensiveness about the spiritual life. When one enters such
a community via even a brief visit to a mosque or for a meal
with a devout family it is easy to see how steady prayerful-
ness can be unselfconscious and natural. Such would have
been the case sixty years ago for many of the inhabitants of
the small Northern Scottish village where I was brought up.
Since then secularisation has emptied the churches there as
elsewhere. Their disappearance coincides with the loss of
regular reminders of the mode of consciousness that is
threatened by literacy and opens the way to individualism.

The Social Construction of Individualism

Theologians abandon religious experience. In his scholarly text
At the Origins of Modern Atheism[25] the Jesuit historian
Michael Buckley presents evidence of the way in which
theologians colluded with their own eclipse during the 17th
century by ceasing to justify belief in its own terms, that is,
religious experience. According to Buckley the seeds of this
mistake lay in a less than careful reading of the greatest of
the scholastic philosophers, the 13th century Dominican
Thomas Aquinas, famed for his 'five ways' of arguing
towards the conclusion that God exists. The way in which
Aquinas' writings are understood has a crucial bearing on
the seriousness with which one takes 'ontological' vs. 'rational' evidence for God, or 'God as immediately given in
experience vs. God as inferentially argued from external

---

[25] New Haven: Yale University Press, 1987. Buckley has since produced a
shorter sequel, *Denying and Disclosing God: the Ambiguous Progress of
Modern Atheism* (Yale, 2004).

evidence'.[26] A close reading of Aquinas' philosophy, says Buckley, shows how he affirms that God is given initially and primordially in direct experience as a presence and not (as many subsequent theologians have taken him to be arguing) simply as the conclusion to a logical argument.

The fateful giving over of the defence of religion to philosophy was an emerging feature of late 16th and early 17th century European thought and appears to have been a response to rumours of widespread atheism within the body politic. Buckley picks out the Flemish Jesuit Leonard Lessius as representative of this view, and notes the oddities in Lessius' argument. Firstly in asserting the ubiquity of atheism he was singularly unable to name contemporary atheists and had to draw upon a list of names from classical antiquity, that is, sixteen hundred years previously. Secondly the individuals he chose were philosophers and not theologians and hence he had defined the problem in philosophical rather than theological terms. Finally the scientists of the period saw themselves as best equipped to defend religion by arguing from the design in impersonal nature. But by making this shift religion ceased to defend itself in its own terms. Buckley expresses the disastrous result,

> For if religion itself has no inherent ground upon which to base its assertion, it is only a question of time until its inner emptiness emerges as positive denial ... Eventually the self denial of religion becomes the more radical but consistent denial that is atheism. If religion has no intrinsic justification, it cannot be justified from the outside. The very forces mustered against atheism will dialectically generate it, just as the northern tribes enlisted to defend Rome and its empire eventually occupied the city and swept the empire away.[27]

The outcome is well known. Two centuries after Lessius, religious apologetics were still couched in the argument from design, for example in the standard university text of the period, William Paley's *Natural Theology*. As we noted earlier Paley's use of the adaptations of living organisms as evidence of a divine designer was soon to be undermined

[26]   *Denying and Disclosing God,* op. cit. p. 51
[27]   *At the Origins of Modern Atheism,* op. cit. p. 360

by Darwin's account in terms of natural selection. The demolition was completed symbolically at the famous (and somewhat apocryphal)[28] debate between Bishop Wilberforce and T.H. Huxley at the British Association meeting in the Oxford Museum in 1860. By insisting on the argument from design as the only valid defence of religious belief, the theologians had connived at their own defeat and handed a weapon to their opponents that is still gleefully used by them to this day, most notably by Richard Dawkins. Buckley quotes James Turner's perceptive comment:

> As I began to trace the origins of unbelief, it slowly dawned on me that the *pattern* I was seeing did not fit conventional expectations, including my own ... Though both science and social transformation loom large in the picture, neither caused unbelief... on the contrary, religion caused unbelief. In trying to adapt their beliefs to socio-economic change, to new moral challenges, to novel problems of knowledge, to the tightening standards of science, the defenders of God slowly strangled Him. If anyone is to be arraigned for deicide, it is not Charles Darwin but his adversary Bishop Samuel Wilberforce ...[29]

When direct appeal to spiritual experience is not merely dismissed but — as is currently the case — diagnosed by senior figures in the psychiatric profession as symptomatic of pathology, or claimed by certain leading scientists to be due to a literal or metaphorical virus infection, the very idea of religious practice suffers a crisis of plausibility. For those who do continue, the climate of uncertainty leads to the temptation to withdraw commitment, performance becomes routine, more and more careless, and eventually the practice may be completely abandoned as a foolish waste of time. The conditions are now set for unrestrained individualism.

Learning to be objective. The loss of immediacy, or the point mode, is no doubt hardly noticed as it is happening. In adult

[28] See J.R. Lucas, 'Wilberforce and Huxley: A Legendary Encounter', *The Historical Journal*, Vol. 22 (2) (1979), pp. 313–30

[29] Quoted in *Denying and Disclosing God,* op.cit. pp. 42–3 and taken from James Turner, *Without God, Without Creed: The Origins of Unbelief in America* (Baltimore: Johns Hopkins University Press, 1986), p. xiii

life we spend most of our time in the line mode, that is, detached from immediate bodily awareness, reflecting about past events and pondering future activities. When for example one is reading about world events in a newspaper it is a commonplace that one's surroundings recede from awareness, remarks addressed to one are not heard, and the comment is often made, 'he's in another world'. If one then positively turns one's attention to the point mode there is a radical shift in awareness involving increased vividness and subtlety in the immediate contents of consciousness. There is nothing wrong — and everything right — about emphasising the need for detachment from immediate bodily feelings when thinking through a complex problem in a scientific or technical field. On the other hand over-pre-occupation with abstract ideas makes people prone to acquiring a disembodied, theoretical consciousness of the self, withdrawn from personal engagement in the immediate environment. At the extreme the psyche of those caught into a cult of detached objectivity, first learned in the school classroom, can take on some of the characteristics of a personality disorder.[30]

An illustration is provided by the difficulties encountered by the American philosopher and psychotherapist Eugene Gendlin[31] when he was approached by academically high flying clients for help. The fact that his consulting

[30] According to the 4th Edition of the Diagnostic and Statistical Manual of the American Psychiatric Association (DSM IV), schizoid personality disorder has the following characteristics:

A pervasive pattern of detachment from social relationships and a restricted range of expression of emotions in interpersonal settings, beginning by early adulthood and present in a variety of contexts, as indicated by four (or more) of the following:

"Neither desires nor enjoys close relationships, including being part of a family; almost always chooses solitary activities. Has little, if any, interest in having sexual experiences with another person; takes pleasure in few, if any, activities. Lacks close friends or confidants other than first-degree relatives; appears indifferent to the praise or criticism of others. Shows emotional coldness, detachment, or flattened affectivity. "

[31] Gendlin's major philosophical work is concerned with the relationship of our immediate bodily experience and meaning making. See Eugene Gendlin, *Experiencing and the Creation of Meaning: A Philosophical and Psychological Approach to the Subjective* (Evanston, Il: Northwestern University Press, 1997).

rooms were adjacent to the main campus of the University of Chicago meant that a fair number of those who sought his advice were in this category. In several cases too good a training in detachment had crippled them by switching off their conscious connection with their feelings. Instead of disclosing their subjective feelings they tended to turn the consultation into an academic debate detached from the immediate sources of their unhappiness.

Gendlin was disconcerted by his failure to assist them and in response he devised a step-by-step methodology that he called 'Focusing'[32] to help such clients to get back into touch with the point mode and the associated bodily feelings. The technique is remarkably similar to that used in traditional religious meditative practice — focusing on a felt sense of the here-and-now — and in fact it has been adapted as a method for teaching contemplative prayer.[33] Gendlin's approach is in tune with a relatively recent general shift in understanding of the indissoluble relation between thought and emotion, pioneered amongst others during the 1990s by the neurologist Antonio Damasio.[34] These developments imply that the detached mode of consciousness so often prized by Western culture[35] may be a socially constructed deviation from the natural form of awareness that has evolved in the human species over many millennia, selected because of its survival value in the total environment.

Another more generally recognised term for the detached and personally abstracted style epitomised by Max Stirner is the one that I have already introduced, 'individualism'.

---

[32] Described in popular format in Gendlin, *Focusing* (Toronto, New York, London, Sydney: Bantam Books, 1981).

[33] This approach was pioneered by two American Catholic priests. See Peter A. Campbell and Edwin M. McMahon, *Biospirituality: A Way to Grow* (Chicago: Loyola University Press, 1997).

[34] See, *Descartes' Error: Emotion, Reason and the Human Brain* (New York: Putnam, 1994); also *The Feeling of What Happens: Body, Emotion and the Making of Consciousness* (London: Vintage Press, 2000); and *Looking for Spinoza: Joy, Sorrow and the Human Brain* (London: William Heinemann, 2003).

[35] I might add that since the loss of immediacy is a particular risk for those who are highly educated this will apply with especial force to the people who control intellectual perspectives and the scientific research agenda.

The word was first coined by Joseph de Maistre in the early 19th century, but its sources are usually thought to have originated much further back in the cultural history of Europe. Among the factors thought to have a bearing are the following:

Religious doctrine. A number of scholars, including Feuerbach himself, have traced the origin as far back as the arrival of Christianity in Europe. In his *Essays on Individualism* the French anthropologist Louis Dumont[36] notes the way that individualistic ideas were certainly present amongst the first Christians, though not in the way the are understood today. The fundamental teaching of Jesus Christ was to see oneself as absolutely unique and of infinite value in the eyes of God, with the corollary that not only I but all other human beings have this status in God's eyes. In the devout community the utter uniqueness of the individual does not threaten social harmony, which is guaranteed by God's oversight, provided people live their lives according to divine law. Dumont thus understands modern secular individualism as remotely but directly inherited from religion, with the crucial difference that the discarding of God leaves secularised individuals free and without divinely ordained social ties. The reference to secularisation places the emergence of the modern form of individualism in the period at or around the Reformation when religious doubt began to appear. In accord with this view, the historian Jacob Burckhardt suggested in a pioneering study[37] that what he called the 'free person' first appeared in renaissance Italy, pre-eminently in renaissance Florence.[38]

---

[36] See, *Essays on Individualism: Modern Ideology in Anthropological Perspective* (Chicago and London: The University of Chicago Press, 1986), especially Chapter 1, 'Genesis' pp. 23–52

[37] See, *The Civilisation of the Renaissance in Italy,* republished in Penguin Classics in 1990.

[38] The privatised subjectivity that Burkhardt noted sounds remarkably like the detachment that Luria saw in collective farm workers once they began to read. Hence one of the factors operating in Florence might have been an increase in literacy.

Another suggested religious source of individualism is in the theology of the Protestant reformer Jean Calvin. The German sociologist Max Weber is probably best known for his suggestion that the spirit of modern capitalism came from the teachings of Calvin,[39] particularly through his emphasis on the doctrine of predestination. The doctrine asserts that from all eternity God has determined the fate of every human being in advance, the saved entering Heaven whilst the reprobate are doomed to languish for ever in Hell. Strictly speaking, according to Calvin's master text *The Institutes of the Christian Religion*, there is nothing one can do, virtuous or sinful, that will affect one's ultimate destiny. Nor is there any way of assuring oneself as to one's final status in the judgement of God.[40] In Weber's view, the doctrine created an unbearable loneliness in the hearts of committed believers that led to pastoral adaptations designed to ease the suffering. The most significant amelioration relative to Weber's theory of the rise of modern capitalism was the idea that a person who prospers materially in this life has probably been blessed by God. As we shall see in a moment, the requirements of the market economy also encouraged the rise of individualism.

Philosophical origins. I have just referred to an epistemological question that preoccupied theologians and in Buckley's opinion derailed apologetics during the 17th century. Another aspect of thought that dominated both the idealist and materialist ends of the spectrum was the solitariness of the individual. On the one hand, in his commitment to reach unassailable certainty Descartes found himself driven back to a position of total isolation with the only undeniable reality his thought, expressed in the most

---

[39] See, *The Protestant Ethic and the Spirit of Capitalism,* trans. Talcott Parsons; intro. R.H. Tawney (London: Unwin University Books, 1930).

[40] When I was a student at Aberdeen University I shared lodgings with a man from the West Highlands of Scotland. He was a Calvinist by conviction, believed he was one of the reprobate (i.e. destined for Hell) and as a result became a drunkard. The antinomian effect of Calvin's doctrines is dramatically represented in James Hogg's classic novel, *The Private Memoirs and Confessions of a Justified Sinner*, first published in 1824.

famous of all philosophical aphorisms '*I think*, therefore I am'. At the other extreme, the materialism of Descartes' English contemporary Thomas Hobbes probably had still more to do with the rise of individualism. It has been argued forcefully that his philosophy continues to influence political and economic practice right up to the present day[41] and it is to this legacy that I now give attention because of its effect on religion.

The date of Hobbes' birth, 5 April 1588, coincided with a moment of national crisis when it was thought that the Spanish Armada was on its way and he, who thought of himself as a timid man, liked to remark that he and fear were twins, born at the same instant. There was certainly plenty of turbulence in his personal life, for he was the son of a ne'er-do-well Anglican parson who had a living near the Wiltshire town of Malmsbury. Eventually, whilst the young man was up at Oxford, Hobbes senior got involved in a fist fight with the vicar of a nearby parish and in disgrace disappeared for good into the anonymity of London. In addition, at the macro level there was enough turmoil in Europe to make anyone feel a degree of apprehension, for the Thirty Years War ravaged the continent throughout Hobbes' early adult life. The fact that he was rumoured (possibly incorrectly)[42] to be an atheist, at a time when atheism was punishable by law may have contributed to the political and personal troubles in which he was immersed and added to his pessimism about human benevolence.

Hobbes constructed a psychological picture of human nature based on his perception of our most basic feature as an endless desire for power. The extent to which we cooperate with other people depends on the degree to which we

---

[41] For a brief account of Hobbes' opinions see, Richard Tuck, *Hobbes* (Oxford University Press, 1989). For more extensive coverage, see *The Cambridge Companion to Hobbes*, ed. Tom Sorrell (Cambridge University Press, 1996).

[42] Hobbes' supposed atheism is the subject of debate. Many scholars, including Richard Tuck, believe he was an atheist. I mentioned earlier the contrary view of A.P. Martinich in his biography, *Hobbes* (London: Routledge, 2005), see pp. 176–207. See also David Berman's fascinating thesis on hidden atheism in, *A History of Atheism in Britain: From Hobbes to Russell* (London & New York: Routledge, 1990).

perceive these interactions to be in our interest.[43] According to Hobbes' most celebrated opinion, life in the state of nature is 'solitary, nasty, brutish and short' and his most famous book, *Leviathan* expounds this view and proposes a way of avoiding this fate. He believed that human beings in general naturally have 'a desire and will to hurt'[44] and talks of 'a generall inclination of all mankind, a perpetuall and restlesse desire of Power after power, that ceaseth onely in Death'.[45] The complete lawlessness means 'that nothing can be Unjust. The notions of Right and Wrong, Justice and Injustice have there no place'.[46] Hobbes' remedy to forestall his terrifying vision is *Leviathan*, a Sovereign who will subdue the anarchy and who himself gains that position in two ways:

> By Natural force; as when a man maketh his children to submit themselves, and their children to his government, as being able to destroy them if they refuse'; or by warre subdueth his enemies to his will, giving them their lives on that condition.[47]

Economics. What has Hobbes' image of human beings 'in a state of nature' to do with the modern world? In 1962 the Canadian economic historian Brough Macpherson proposed an answer to that question. According to him, Hobbes' account of society continues to dictate the organisation of the modern bureaucratic state and is based, in

---

[43] In this sense he was a precursor of modern attempts of biologists to explain altruism as refined selfishness, via the theories of reciprocal altruism and kin selection (see the books by Cronin and Wright, op. cit. in the notes to Chapter One).

[44] In, *Philosophical Rudiments concerning Government and Society*, Ch. 1, Section 4, 25–26, (quoted in MacPherson 1962: p. 44).

[45] *Leviathan*, edited with an introduction by C.B. Macpherson (London: Penguin Classics, 1985), p. 161 Bernard Gert refers to this remark in his review of Hobbes' psychology and claims that the alarming rhetoric distracts the reader from grasping his rather more benign view of human nature. Maybe so, but most commentators *have* been thus distracted, and it is their influence that has constructed the common understanding of Hobbes. See, Bernard Gert, 'Hobbes' psychology', in *The Cambridge Companion to Hobbes*, ed. Tom Sorell (Cambridge University Press, 1996), p. 168

[46] *Ibid.*, p. 188

[47] *Ibid.*, p. 228

Macpherson's phrase, on 'possessive individualism'.[48] An important aspect of this perspective is the belief that individuals are proprietors of their own bodies, with the further implication that their constitution owes nothing to the surrounding society. In the market economy their relationship to one another is commercial; their bodily labours become commodities that can be sold like any other commodity.[49] Macpherson's belief was that Hobbes' doctrine was conditioned by the social order that was beginning to emerge; that is to say, 17th century bourgeois society at the point where market forces first began to take on a dominant role.[50] This fourth and most crucial step in the construction of European individualism massively increasing the legitimacy of the idea, because it was to come to be seen eventually as the key to economic stability on a global scale.

It is important to underline once more the point that there was nothing new in the desire for possessions, or in the use of violence to further greed. The novelty was that avarice began to be seen as a necessary expedient and indeed a virtue, in the search for economic and political stability. The economic historian Albert Hirschman has given what now

---

[48]   C.B. Macpherson, *The Political Theory of Possessive Individualism* (Oxford Uniiversity Press, 1962).

[49]   For a discussion of Macpherson's account of proprietorship of the body, see Adam Carter's article, 'Of property and the human: or C.B. Macpherson, Samuel Hearne and Contemporary Theory', *University of Toronto Quarterly* 74 (3), 2004, 829–44

[50]   Macpherson's thesis was immediately the subject of controversy. Some scholars contend that his argument was refuted in a 1965 article by Keith Thomas in which he demonstrated convincingly that Hobbes' personal sympathies were not with the bourgeoisie but rather with the aristocracy, perhaps unsurprisingly, since the source of his living for much of his adult life was as tutor to the Cavendish family in Hardwick Hall, one of the great mansion houses of England. See, Keith Thomas, 'The social origins of Hobbes' political thought', in *Hobbes Studies*, ed. K.C. Brown (Oxford: Blackwell, 1965). In his assessment of Macpherson's academic achievement, Jules Townsend claims that the criticism is wrongheaded and notes that in a reply to Thomas, Macpherson pointed out that he was not concerned with Hobbes' personal motivation, but with his unstated (and possibly unconscious) assumptions about the then emerging possessive market society. See Jules Townshend, *C.B. Macpherson and the Problem of Liberal Democracy* (Edinburgh University Press, 2000), especially, Chapter 2. See also Macpherson's introduction to the Penguin edition of *Leviathan*, published in 1968.

looks like the classic account of this process in his book *The Passions and the Interests*.[51] He notes how during the Renaissance thoughtful people began to feel that religion was losing its moral authority as a restraint on human destructiveness and sought for other means of social control. By the 17th century, as we have seen, Hobbes' alarm led him to propose in *Leviathan* the need for a tyrant to suppress uncontrolled violence by the threat of his own superior force of arms. But who, in turn, is to restrain the brutalities of the sovereign?

According to Hirschman, the ingenious solution that began to gain general consensus during the 17th and 18th century was to set up the desire for personal gain in opposition to the other passions. The great value of avarice was its predictability, for there was widespread agreement that unlike other passions such as anger or sexual desire which come and go, the lust for possessions operates to the same degree at all times and in all people. However, if it was to be made acceptable there had to be a process of 'sanitization', for in everyday life outside the field of economics, avarice was still considered a revolting sin. The term that legitimised it and came into greater and greater use was 'interest' and with this semantic shift it literally took on the mantle of a virtue. The steady dependability of self-interest set it reassuringly apart from the flightiness of the other passions.[52]

The importance of predictability meant that 'interest' was finally given the status of the pivot of the market by Adam Smith, the founder of modern economics, in his most famous work *The Wealth of Nations*, published in 1776.[53] In a celebrated passage, Smith remarks,

---

[51] *The Passions and the Interests: Political Arguments for Capitalism before its Triumph* (Princeton University Press, 1977), republished in 1977 as a Twentieth Anniversary Edition with a foreword by Amartya Sen.

[52] In 1767 the Scottish economist Sir James Steuart argued that in economic matters, '…were a people to become quite disinterested: there would be no possibility of governing them. Everyone might consider the interest of his country in a different light, and many might join in the ruin of it, by endeavoring to promote its advantages.' (quoted in Hirschman, p. 50)

[53] Currently available as a two-volume paperback edited by Andrew Skinner and published in 1999 by Penguin Books.

.... man has almost constant occasion for the help of his brethren, and it is in vain for him to expect it of their benevolence only. He will be more likely to prevail if he can interest their self-love in his favour, and show them that it is for their own advantage to do for him what he requires of them. Whoever offers to another a bargain of any kind, proposes to do this. Give me that which I want, and you shall have this which you want, is the meaning of every such offer; and it is in this manner that we obtain from one another the far greater part of those good offices which we stand in need of. It is not from the benevolence of the butcher, the brewer, or the baker that we expect our dinner, but from their regard to their own interest. We address ourselves not to their humanity but to their self-love, and never talk to them of our own necessities but of their advantages.[54]

Egotism and the Final Repudiation of Relational Consciousness

It was Adam Smith, says Hirschman, who gave a financial rather than a political or moral justification for the unrestricted pursuit of personal gain.[55] The individualist philosophies to which I referred earlier, when allied to the promotion of self-interest as the necessary basis for a stable market economy, formed a hugely powerful alliance. We in the contemporary Western world are the inheritors of the consequences, the enfeebling of relational consciousness, blindness to the spiritual dimension of life, and hence also a puzzlement and sense of implausibility surrounding religion.

During the 19th century this same series of developments gave birth to the personal convictions of Max Stirner, whose

---

[54] *Ibid.*, pp. 118–9

[55] A distinction must be made between Smith's account of the way things are in capitalist society and his personal view of ethics. Smith's moral philosophy is expounded in *The Theory of Moral Sentiments* (1759) published seventeen years before *The Wealth of Nations*. He has much to say of 'sympathy' which suggests that it is not remote from relational consciousness. The apparent ethical disjunction between the two works has led to much discussion. It must be added that Smith's rhetoric, particularly in the later chapters of *The Wealth of Nations* frequently makes clear his distaste for some of the situations he is describing (See, Muller, 1993).

language when he refers to other people is reminiscent of Hobbes at his loneliest:

> For me you are nothing but my food, even as I am fed upon and turned to use by you. We have only one relation to each other, that of *usableness,* of utility, of use.[56]

And elsewhere,

> I do not allow myself to be disturbed in my self-enjoyment. I practise a Terrorism of the Self, which drives off every human consideration. I think nothing of Nature, men and their laws, human society and its love, and I sever every general connection with it, even that of language. To all the demands of your Ought, to all the demands of your categorical judgment, I oppose the ataraxy of my Ego.[57]

In his biography of Stirner, R.W.K Paterson[58] remarks on the explosive effect of Stirner's book on his neo-Hegelian colleagues, who either were blind to the point he was making or lacked the courage to follow where it led. Logically they ought to have seen that not just God, but all 'transcendental objects' were merely projections, but the implied abandonment of every moral principal was so radical that they stopped short and, from Stirner's point of view, continued to be unconsciously and piously religious. The brutality potentially unleashed by an acceptance of his rationale is exactly what Hobbes had described in his account of man in a state of nature without restraint on the obligation not to steal, lie, or kill if need be, to ensure that one's own interests are protected.

I like to imagine the scene in Hippel's wine bar on a mythical evening when the little group finally realised what Stirner was up to and their jaws dropped. For one thing, it gave *carte blanche* to the class enemy, the capitalist fat cat who had been described by Marx as 'wholly preoccupied with his private interest and acting in accordance with his private caprice' and for whom 'the only bond between men

---

[56] *Ibid.*, pp. 296–7.
[57] Quoted in Paterson, p. 184
[58] *The Nihilistic Egoist Max Stirner* published for the University of Hull by Oxford University Press in 1971.

is natural necessity, need and private interest'.[59] We have seen that 'interest' is a cleaned up synonym for avarice or greed, as was made explicit in the film *Wall Street* by the entrepreneur Gordon Gecko in his chilling defence of the axiom 'greed is good'.[60] That film is fiction and so can perhaps be dismissed, but appeals to greed are widespread in the advertising industry (cf. the billboards appearing in 2005 in the United Kingdom, advertising Lynx Deodorant with giant letters announcing that 'Greed is Good!')

Individualism undermined the moral basis for interchange in the marketplace. As Macpherson remarked, the binding obligation that remains in possessive market societies is to make sure the market does not collapse through financial mismanagement. In this circumstance the difference between moral obligation and what is financially prudent becomes insignificant. Individualism also potentially undermined capitalism's great rival, communism, and condemned it to a similar moral vacuum, as Karl Marx was quick to grasp. When he first read *The Ego and His Own,* Friedrich Engels thought it was rather a good book and commended it to Marx, who was immediately enraged by it. He saw where it was leading and needed to squash it, but it seems he was at a loss as to how best to do the deed.

Engels did not take much persuading to change his mind and in 1845 the two of them began writing what became *The German Ideology*,[61] initially intended as a critique of Feuerbach but Marx's rage got the better of him and the main theme of the book, several hundred pages long, is a fusillade of insults directed towards Stirner. The sense of an out-of-control overkill suggests that, at some level, Marx felt cornered. His dilemma was caused by his need to justify the predicted proletarian revolution on moral grounds that Stirner dismissed as mere projections no different in kind than religious belief. It seems that Marx felt unable to

[59] Quoted in Michael Walzer (1990). 'The communitarian critique of liberalism', *Political Theory*, 18 (1), 6–23.

[60] Starring Michael Douglas in the role of Gordon Gecko. Directed by Oliver Stone, written by Stanley Weiser and Oliver Stone.

[61] Engels, *The German Ideology* (Amherst, New York: Prometheus Books, 1998).

defend his own ideals against Stirner's logic and resorted to bluster. Whether Marx remained at heart a moralist and believer in a human spiritual essence is a matter for scholarly argument.[62] What is not in dispute is the fact that after the publication of Stirner's book Marx's statements on the future of the revolution are notable for the way they avoid an appeal to morality and replace it with the inevitability of the onward roll of the impersonal dialectic of history. From within the logic of neo-Hegelianism it seems that Stirner's egotist anarchism had effectively won the day.

Stirner is regarded in some circles as a hero. His first biographer, John Henry Mackay[63] was an uncritical admirer, making the grandiose prediction that *The Ego and His Own* would come to replace the Bible as the supreme guide to human conduct. Various authors have contended that Stirner was a forerunner of existentialism, of Neitzsche,[64] of Freud's emancipation of the ego in psychoanalysis and of the postmodern dismissal of ideology[65] and hence the rise of relativism. He is commended as giving personal freedom to many by allowing them to escape from the bonds of the Superego. There is a degree of truth in this view, especially in relation to the crippling restrictions put on freedom of expression by the institutions of the state and the church during the 19th century. Nevertheless, I conclude that Stirner was fatally damaged as a human being by the very egotism he advocated. The difficulty for Stirner is that he has entirely lost touch with his own biologically built-in relational consciousness. He writes as someone almost

---

[62] See, for example, Lobkowicz, N. (1969). 'Karl Marx and Max Stirner', in, *Demythologizing Marxism*, ed. Frederick J. Adelmann (Beacon Hill: Boston College); Norman Geras, *Marx and Human Nature: Refutation of a Legend* (London: Verso, 1983); also Lawrence Wilde, *Ethical Marxism and its Radical Critics* (London: Macmillan Press, 1998).

[63] See, *Max Stirner: His Life and Work*, trans. Hubert Kennedy (Concord, CA: Peremptory Publications, 2005).

[64] See John Carroll, *Break-Out from the Crystal Palace. The anarcho-psychological critique: Stirner, Neitzsche, Dostoevsky* (London and Boston: Routledge and Kegan Paul, 1974).

[65] See Saul Newman, 'Spectres of Stirner: a contemporary critique of ideology', *Journal of Political Ideologies*, 6 (1), 2001, 309–30. Newman calls Stirner a 'post-structuralist' with views akin to Michel Foucault.

completely blind to the call of another person on his moral resources, such as is described in the work of Emmanuel Levinas.[66] His obtuseness suggests the symptoms of a personality disorder, as indeed is implied in a commentary on Stirner's ideas by the philosopher and contemplative, Martin Buber. Buber labels him a sociopath:

> He simply does not know what of elemental reality lies between life and life, he does not know the mysteries of address and answer, claim and disclaim, word and response... [67]

There is another equally grave danger created by the cult of individualism. As Hobbes pointed out in *Leviathan*, the more thoroughgoing the individualism, the more necessary is a tyrant to ensure that the structure of the total society does not collapse. Traditional social capital, the bond of loving friendship that builds up in stable communities, has no formal place and is replaced by totalitarian means of social control. Totalitarianism is the logical endpoint for a society that has lost touch with relational consciousness. Buber makes the same point in his insight into the role of extreme individualism in the creation of the authoritarianisms of the political Right and Left.

> 'True is what is mine' are formulas which forecast a congealing of the soul unsuspected by Stirner in all his rhetorical assurance. But also many a rigid collective *We* set in, which rejects a superior authority, is easily understood as a translation from the speech of the Unique One into that of the *it* which acknowledges nothing but itself — carried out against Stirner's intention, who hotly opposes any plural version.[68]

Nazism and the authoritarian Marxism of Stalin are historically recent examples of translations of Stirner's One into the collective *We*, but the motivations underlying much contemporary religious, political and sporting violence are also arguably the unhappy fruits of individualism. In the case of fundamentalist religious sects the polarization of the

---

[66] See *The Levinas Reader*, ed. , Sean Hand (Oxford: Blackwell, 1989).
[67] *Ibid.*, p. 66
[68] *Ibid.*, p. 61

world into good and evil empires and the consequent disregard for human life indicates a tragic disengagement from the relational consciousness that underlies genuine religion. The political consequences of this dismissal of spiritual awareness are very great, and around us in full measure at the present time.

In the end, the most telling judgement on Stirner comes from the person who was most closely in touch with his practical attempt to live according to his egotist convictions. After two and a half years of marriage, during which Stirner purloined her substantial dowry and frittered it away, Marie Dahnhardt decided that enough was enough and she left him. Further adventures eventually led her into the arms of the Christianity that Stirner had so utterly repudiated.

In 1897 Stirner's biographer John Mackay managed to track down Marie in her convent in London and attempted to interview her. She flatly refused to meet him and sent him a statement announcing that she had cut herself off entirely from what she described as Stirner's slyness and the lovelessness of their marriage. A search of her belongings after her death did not disclose a single vestige of her youth in Berlin. Mackay was appalled by Marie's disloyalty to his hero, but presumably on Stirner's own egotist principles there was no reason for him to be upset. Marie had simply gone her own way. My guess is that when she looked back on her relationship with Max she wondered how she could have been so foolish, for she had temporarily bought in to European individualism in its most extreme form or, as Stirner's critics pointed out, the paradoxical commitment to selfishness as an ideal.

Chapter Four

Empirical Science Meets Empirical Religion

> So now since eighteen months ago the dawn, three months ago the proper light of day, and indeed a very few days ago the pure Sun itself of the most marvellous contemplation has shone forth—nothing holds me; I will indulge my sacred fury; I will taunt mankind with the candid confession that I have stolen the golden vases of the Egyptians, in order to build of them a tabernacle to my God, far indeed from the bounds of Egypt. If you forgive me, I shall rejoice; if you are angry, I shall bear it; the die is cast, the book is written, whether to be read now or by posterity I care not; it may wait a hundred years for its reader, if God himself has waited six thousand years for a man to contemplate his work.[1]

Imagine a traveller arriving in Western Europe for the first time, let's say in London. Let's decide that he's male, that is, a member of the gender that tends to have particular difficulty with religion in the West. It doesn't matter where he has come from, but it might as well be from another planet for he knows absolutely nothing of the cultural history that has shaped the way these Europeans make sense of life. A fairy has strolled up from the bottom of the garden and waved a wand ensuring that this man has nevertheless

---

[1] The 16th-century cosmologist Kepler, quoted by Michael Polanyi in his Gifford Lectures in Aberdeen University for the session 1951–2. See, *Personal Knowledge: Towards a Post-Critical Philosophy* (University of Chicago Press, 1958), p. 7.

acquired a set of technical skills including a scientific training, philosophical assumptions that are those of a critical realist[2] and a conviction that the origin of species has come about through the process of natural selection.

The visitor also resembles around 75% of the adult population of Britain in being aware of a transcendent dimension to his experience.[3] Unlike most British people, though in agreement with the great majority of *Homo sapiens* he has integrated transcendence into the fabric of his life via the religious culture to which he belongs. Back home on the other planet religion is like the weather. Religion may be gloriously beautiful, threateningly ugly, or just plain dull, but the idea that it could be abolished is as ridiculous as doing away with the sky. Until arriving in Britain this visitor didn't even know that people could seriously advocate such a thing.

Thus he is astonished when he lands at Heathrow in 2006 and, having run the gauntlet of immigration and customs, calls in at an airport bookstore to see what people are reading (by another miracle he can speak fluent English). Prominently displayed on the shelves is Richard Dawkins' book *The God Delusion* which has been one of the top five nonfiction best-sellers for many weeks. Meanwhile, John Lennon's ever popular 'Imagine' is playing soothingly in the background:

> Imagine there's no countries
> It isn't hard to do
> Nothing to kill or die for
> And no religion too

---

[2]   Critical realism makes the commonsense assumption that the world is really there and is not a product of our imagination. However, because of our human limitations (presuppositions of our culture, lack of practical tools for the job, limited intellect etc.) we never have complete knowledge about reality. The scientific method, depending directly on the investigation of empirical data is assumed to be the surest way of getting somewhere near the truth.

[3]   For the national survey and statistical data, see David Hay and Kate Hunt, *The Spirituality of People who don't go to Church* (Nottingham University Research Report, 2000). For a full discussion of the research, see my book *Something There: The Biology of the Human Spirit* (Darton, Longman & Todd, 2006).

Imagine all the people
Living life in peace ...

You may say I'm a dreamer
But I'm not the only one
I hope someday you'll join us
And the world will be as one[4]

It is because of his imaginativeness that this man has always been fascinated by both science and religion, which he sees as the two great practical ways of exploring the remarkable reality in which we human beings find ourselves. So why do Westerners want to get rid of the religious part of the search? A quick skim through *The God Delusion* is enough to give our visitor the general idea. Perhaps Dawkins is right.

The visitor is an open-minded sort, so once he has settled in and begun to get used to the new environment, he decides to read up on this question. With a strong belief in the power of the scientific method he is bound to see empirical data as highly relevant to his enquiries. Not having much time he avoids philosophical and theological material and sticks to major and recent scientific literature dealing with what is going on in the body when someone undertakes the commonest of all practical religious exercises, meditation or prayer. In the process he uncovers three dominant issues:

Recent Developments in Understanding the Neurophysiology of the Brain

Since the early 1970s when Godfrey Hounsfield invented the computed tomographic (CT) scanner and the principles of functional Magnetic Resonance Imaging (fMRI) were worked out, it has been possible to take photographs of soft tissue inside a living body. Only very recently (at the time of writing, within the past ten years) have developments of these methods begun to uncover what is happening in the brain when someone undertakes meditation or contemplative prayer. The most interesting research to date is that directed initially by the late Eugene d'Aquili and subse-

[4]   From the album *Imagine*, released October 11, 1971 by Parlophone

quently by his colleague Andrew Newberg in the Department of Nuclear Medicine at the University of Pennsylvania
in Philadelphia.[5]

D'Aquili and Newberg had been curious for some time
about the physiological basis for transcendent experience[6]
and their pioneering research was with experts in Tibetan
Buddhist meditation. Subsequently Newberg and his colleagues repeated the study with a group of Franciscan nuns
who practice 'centering prayer'. Though the religious rationale for their practice was different, both the Buddhists and
the Catholic nuns had the same purpose of staying as attentively as possible in the here-and-now either by being aware
of the breathing, or by placing themselves in the presence of
God. The researchers used a SPECT scanner, which is a
development of the CT scanner that can detect the movement of fluids in soft tissue, usually by injecting a radioac-
tive isotope into the bloodstream. In this way they were able
to compare patterns of blood flow in the brains of the
meditators when they were not meditating (the baseline
state) and when they had entered a state of deep meditation.[7] Newberg discovered that there were numerous
changes happening in different parts of the brain during the
shift from the baseline to the meditative state, and that in
many ways the Buddhists and the nuns exhibited parallel
dynamic patterns.

The most dramatic changes were in the blood supply to
the parietal lobes and the frontal lobes of the cerebral cortex
and in the thalamus. In the meditative state there is a reduc-
tion of blood flow to the parietal region and an increased
flow to the frontal lobes. This is a remarkable finding

[5]   See, Andrew Newberg, Eugene d'Aquili and Vince Rause, *Why God Won't
      Go Away: Brain Science and the Biology of Belief* (New York: Ballantine Books,
      2001); also, Newberg and Waldman's *Why We Believe What We Believe:
      Uncovering Our Biological Need for Meaning, Spirituality, and Truth* (New
      York: Free Press, 2006).

[6]   See their first joint book on the subject, *The Mystical Mind: Probing the
      Biology of Religious Experience* (Augsberg Press, 1999).

[7]   Technical details are available in Newberg and Iverson's paper, 'The
      neural basis of the complex mental task of meditation: neurotransmitter
      and neurochemical considerations', *Medical Hypotheses*, 61 (2) (2003),
      282–91.

because it represents a physiological confirmation of centuries of subjective accounts of mystical experience across many religious cultures.

The parietal lobes have as one of their functions the job of telling us where we are in space by creating a three dimensional picture of the world around us. When blood moves away from there, the experience is of a loss of the distinction between the self and the rest of reality. At the same time the increased activity in the frontal lobes leads to a greatly increased level of awareness. A third change is an increase of activity in the thalamus, which lies deep inside the brain, just above the brain stem, and controls the flow of incoming sensory information. The outcome of these alterations is the experience that the isolated self is replaced by the sense that all is One, combined with an intensely enhanced experience of reality – the conviction of being in touch with ultimate reality.

The differences between the nuns and the Buddhists appear to be connected with their contrasting systems of belief, and therefore their conscious intentions when they settle down to their religious exercises. Newberg noted increases in the blood flow to the right hemisphere and more specifically the language centre in the case of the nuns, probably because the form of prayer they used involved understanding the meanings of words. The Buddhists on the other hand were focusing on a sacred image and consequently exhibited an increased blood flow in the region of the inferior temporal lobes, the parts of the brain concerned with processing vision.

Newberg and his colleagues are not the only researchers concerned with the relationship between practical religious exercises like meditation and brain state. Mario Beauregard and Vincent Paquette at the University of Montreal have attempted a somewhat similar exercise with a group of volunteer Carmelite nuns, in this case using an MRI scanner.[8] Since MRI scanners operate on a completely different prin-

---

[8]   See, Mario Beauregard and Vincent Paquette, 'Neural correlates of a mystical experience in Carmelite nuns', *Neuroscience Letters* 405 (2006), 186–190.

ciple from SPECT scanners it is necessary to be cautious in drawing comparisons. In addition the Montreal researchers required their subjects to undertake a fundamentally different task from Newberg's volunteers. Beauregard asked the nuns to recall as vividly as possible a moment of intense religious experience from the past, whilst their brains were being monitored in the scanner and recollection may involve different neurophysiological processes from those occurring when doing a task directly. Nevertheless, it is clear that there were detectable alterations in brain activity and there was a considerable overlap in the points in the brain where these activities took place. On a rather different tack, Nina Azari[9] of the University of Hawaii has also made investigations of a group of fundamentalist Protestant Christians whilst the were in what they themselves described as a religious state, using PET scanning apparatus. There was activation of the parts of the brain concerned with cognition, but also their experience *felt* religious.

To our hypothetical visitor from another planet, with his keen commitment to the importance of empirical data, this research programme, though at an early stage, quite clearly and unequivocally demonstrates that there are physical events occurring in the brain in parallel with the mental events of praying and meditating. The data thus totally contradict the assertion of the father figure of modern atheism, Ludwig Feuerbach. He explicitly stated during a famous series of lectures in 1848 in Heidelberg[10] that there is no organ of religious experience and that claims to such experience are based on delusional fantasy and stupidity. Feuerbach's assertion was more or less the default position of atheists for the next hundred years, although even when

[9]   See, Nina P. Azari and Dieter Birnbacher, 'The role of cognition and feeling in religious experience', *Zygon* 39 (4) (2004), 901–18.

[10] Published in 1851 as *Lectures on the Essence of Religion*. Translation by Ralph Manheim (New York and London: Harper & Row in New York and London, 1967), see especially pp. 219 –21. It is not quite true to say that Feuerbach was the first to make the claim explicitly. Kant makes a rather similar assertion in *Religion Within the Limits of Reason Alone* (1793). See the translation by Theodore M Greene & Hoyt H. Hudson (New York: Harper & Row, 1960), p. 163.

he gave his Heidelberg lectures there was already evidence
of a possible physiological link. The first hint that this might
be so came from a medical report on the religiosity of epileptics by the French medical scientist Jean Etienne Esquirol in
1838. Since then there have been repeated accounts of religious experience occurring in some temporal lobe epileptics just before the onset of a fit and that the experience is
remarkable by its intensity. However the frequency of such
experience amongst epileptics does not seem to be significantly different from the general population.[11]

Another researcher who has taken an interest in the role
of the temporal lobe in religious experience is Michael
Persinger, in the Laurentian University in Sudbury,
Ontario. Persinger thinks that the cause of such experience
is a temporary electrical seizure in the temporal lobe produced by geophysical movements of the earth that in turn
create electrical impulses that impact on the brain. This last
hypothesis seems to me to be so speculative as to verge on
the eccentric, though to be fair to Persinger it looks as if it
might be empirically testable, at least in principle. He has
taken the step of inventing a helmet which can send
micro-electric impulses into the appropriate part of the
brain and in about 40% of cases his experimental subjects
report a variety of phenomena including a sense of presence, in the shape of ghosts, fairies, demons, angels
and — why not — God himself. Persinger is another
researcher who claims to be even-handed but his style of
presentation is to say the least, mechanistic. For example he
foresees a time when his machine will be able to switch on
mystical visions at will to assist depressed people, though
he worries that it could also be used by the unscrupulous to
motivate them to commit crimes.

Behind this kind of statement lie a number of unstated
philosophical assumptions, one of which is that the halluci-

---

[11] See, Tom Sensky et al. paper on 'The interictal personality traits of
temporal lobe epileptics: Religious belief and its association with reported
mystical experiences' in RJ. Porter et al. (eds.), *Advances in Epileptology:
XVth Epilepsy International Symposium* (New York: Raven Press, 1984),
pp. 545–9.

natory experience of temporal lobe epileptics or of people subjected to artificial stimulation of the temporal lobes is no different ontologically from supposed genuine transcendence. A second assumption is that the experience of transcendence is indicative of nothing more than pathology, since it appears to be produced in exaggerated form in people suffering from epilepsy. Neither of these assumptions is justified by Persinger and both imply a prior acceptance of a reductionist model of the human being.

In everyday life we are constantly making distinctions between artificially induced hallucination and reality. Many perfectly ordinary and uncontroversial experiences like seeing people across a room or hearing the murmur of voices from next door can be reproduced in the hallucinations of those who are mentally ill and no one thinks twice about discriminating between the two. Furthermore every undergraduate who has read an introductory textbook of neurophysiology knows of the work of Wilder Penfield[12] on identifying the neurological bases of perception by artificially stimulating the surface of the cerebral cortex. Penfield triggered hallucinations corresponding to the function of the part of the cortex he stimulated, and on that basis produced the familiar diagrams showing the distribution of those functions. No one in the workaday world assumes that the production of hallucinations implies that normal sensory experience is therefore hallucinatory. Common sense suggests that there is something arbitrary about accepting the validity of distinguishing between reality and hallucination in the case of Penfield's experiments whilst refusing to apply the same ontological criteria to spiritual or religious experience.

The arbitrariness is based on no more than a philosophical assumption about the nature of reality and our interplanetary visitor would, I think, be puzzled by the confidence with which this is asserted. It would be perfectly obvious to him that you can produce hallucinations with

---

[12] See for example, Wilder Penfield and Theodore Rasmussen's text, *The cerebral cortex of man : a clinical study of localization of function* (New York: Macmillan, 1950).

the use of electrodes. The finding that this is so certainly raises profound questions about ontology in general, but even the most ivory towered theorist about these matters operates on the commonsense assumption that our ordinary experience is, in general, reliable. If it were not, natural selection would have put an end to us long ago. The visitor comes from a culture where the encounter with transcendence is considered normal, and like every other kind of experience it provides in general, reliable information, although as in every other field there are specialists whose role it is to help in discriminating between the genuine and the delusional. He has no knowledge of the sceptical turn in thought produced by the historical and economic forces I discussed in the previous chapter. Therefore when he hears sceptics talking, though they sound reasonable enough by their own criteria, he finds them implausible when measured by his total experience of life.

The Genetics of Transcendence

In a quite separate empirical approach to the nature of spiritual experience, the visitor would discover data that parallel the findings of neurophysiologists like Newberg. One of the most impressive pieces of research is a twin study reported by Katherine Kirk and her colleagues in 1999. [13]Identical or monozygotic twins' characteristics are genetically the same, whilst dizygotics are as different from each other as ordinary brothers and sisters. These facts make it possible to use statistical techniques to find out the extent to which certain aspects of human behaviour and awareness are genetically or environmentally determined. The technique has been in use for many years and nowadays many academic institutions maintain 'twin banks' made up of volunteers who are willing to participate as subjects in this kind of research. Until recently no one had thought of looking directly at the inheritance of spiritual awareness, proba-

[13]   See, Kirk, K., Martin, N. & Eaves, L., 'Self-transcendence as a measure of spirituality in a sample of older Australia twins', *Twin Research* 2 (2) (1999), 81–7.

bly because of assumptions similar to those of Feuerbach. It was also the case that researchers in this area often failed to make a conceptual distinction between different categories of religious behaviour such as had been made by the psychologist Gordon Allport in his studies of 'intrinsic' and 'extrinsic' religion.[14] Approximately, people in Allport's extrinsic category practice their religion for social reasons e.g. it is the done thing in one's community, or it is the way to get ahead, or a means of meeting people. or (as is currently the case in Britain) it is diplomatically wise to participate in services in one's local church if one is hoping to get one's child a place in a church school. For intrinsics religion is personally important, it provides meaning and a rule of life. It seems possible that the latter category is more connected with heredity than the former.

Kirk and her fellow workers were able to look at this question because during the 1980s an American psychiatrist called Robert Cloninger devised a scale for the measurement of 'self transcendence'. Cloninger had in mind three aspects of experience that apply very directly to people who practise religious exercises like prayer and meditation:

- *Self forgetfulness* — the ability to lose oneself in a task to the extent that it appears to 'do itself', reminiscent of the condition described by Mihaly Csikszentmihalyi as 'flow'.[15] Flow had been linked with practical religion in Isabella Csikszentmihalyi's study of the Jesuit spiritual exercises[16] as an attempt to generate flow in the whole of life, which may be another way of expressing the Ignatian precept 'to see God in all things'.

- *Transpersonal identification* — the experience of the disappearance of the distinction between the self and the rest of reality, as referred to above in relation to mystical experience. Here there is a clear link with the finding of Newberg and his colleagues that the metabolic rate is

[14] See Allport's *The Individual and His Religion* (New York: Macmillan, 1962).

[15] See, for example, Csikszentmihalyi, M., *Beyond Boredom and Anxiety* (San Francisco: Jossey-Bass, 1975).

[16] See, Csikszentmihalyi, I., 'Flow in a historical context: the case of the Jesuits' in Mihaly Csikszentmihalyi and Isabella Csikszentmihalyi (eds), *Psychological Studies of Flow in Consciousness* (New York: Cambridge University Press, 1988).

reduced in the posterior superior parietal lobes on entering deep meditation.

- *Mysticism* — a direct reference to mystical experience; being concerned and interested in the deepest mysteries of existence and hence concerned with the practicalities of investigating transcendence. People with this kind of interest are likely to fall into Gordon Allport's category of the intrinsically religious as opposed to the extrinsically religious.

When they looked at the scores of the sample of Australian twins, Kirk and her fellow workers found that the practice of going to church was primarily a matter of learning from one's family or local community what was expected in terms of correct behaviour. It had very little to do with any kind of genetic inheritance. On the other hand identical twins were twice as likely to get similar scores on Cloninger's scale compared with non-identical twins. This strongly suggests that differences in the ability to self- transcend are significantly affected by one's genetic make up.

In addition to Kirk's investigation there have been subsequent twin studies published by Gillespie, Cloninger and colleagues in 2003[17] and a Japanese team led by Juko Ando in 2004 both showing scores on transcendence to be heavily determined by heredity. In other words, from a Darwinian perspective, it looks very much as if the skills of self-transcendence have been selected for in the process of evolution because they have survival value. It is of course too early to say whether these pieces of research are indicative of a general feature of the human genome, but the fact that the research led by Ando was with a Japanese sample does indicate agreement across cultures. Taken together with what we know from cross-cultural studies of religious practices it seems highly plausible that we are looking at a human

---

[17] Nathan Gillespie, Robert Cloninger et al., 'The genetic and environmental relationship between Cloninger's dimensions of temperament and character', *Personality and Individual Differences* 35 (2003), 1931–46; also, Juko Ando et al., 'Genetic and environmental structure of Cloninger's temperament and character dimensions', *Journal of Personality Disorders* 18 (4) (2004), 379–93.

universal, as was predicted by Alister Hardy.[18] When our hypothetical interplanetary visitor came across the data, even as they stand, they would be perfectly consonant with his own assumptions. Yet in the Western world those assumptions until recently would without doubt have been dismissed by a large proportion of the scientific community. That this is less likely today is no doubt in part due to the accumulation of empirical evidence which is making it more and more implausible to cling on to Feuerbach's rejection of a biological element in religion.

Even fiercely hostile opponents of religion sometimes feel forced to accept that it can have a positive function from an evolutionary perspective. We have seen that Richard Dawkins compares religion to a virus infection. At the same time he turns to the speculations of Boyer and Atran that religious beliefs are based on the prior evolution of cognitive structures for quite separate purposes, then utilised in irrational ways also turn out to have survival value. My guess is that our visitor would be somewhat bewildered by this line of reasoning, for whilst it makes logical sense if one were trying to explain away something, why are these critics so anxious to explain it away?

Religion and Violence

The visitor would soon realise that a major reason for dislike is the fearfulness of the potential destructiveness of religious fanaticism I mentioned earlier. Religion certainly has the ability to catalyse violence, and there is no arguing against the savagery that has been unloosed in the past or in our own time and justified in religious terms. This is so repulsive and so unhappily true that I can sympathise with one of my furious correspondents on the Internet who wrote, 'There is not a religion in this world that does not write its history in the blood of innocent people'.

How would the intergalactic visitor respond to the accusation? I think he would agree with the accusers but go on to ask a more fundamental question concerning whether reli-

[18]   See his Gifford Lectures in Aberdeen University, Op. cit.

gion is inherently more vulnerable to corruption and violence than any other large scale and widespread social
institution that matters to people — let's say for example politics or the law or the economic system. The commonsense
answer is that these factors amongst many others are in a
complex relationship that is difficult or impossible to disen-
tangle. Religiously well-informed writers on questions of
peace and war do not seek to repudiate religion's potential
for truly horrendous acts of violence, but recognize that
dimensions of life that matter deeply to people always have
the possibility of stimulating violence. Authors like Scott
Appleby or Michael Burleigh in their analyses of the complexities of the troubles in Northern Ireland, the Balkans,
and the Middle East[19] have the wit to know that any large
scale human endeavour is corruptible. Hence blanket
condemnation of the type employed by Sam Harris and
Richard Dawkins is almost certainly a sign of ignorance and
oversimplification.

The lack of political realism on the part of secularist critics
of the role of religion in these conflicts is illustrated by their
failure to realise that as religion contributes to the conflict, it
is only through a proper and empathic understanding of
religion that reconciliation can be created. Scott Appleby
detects two main causes of the religious violence that runs
counter to the longing for peace. He notes firstly poor
education in the core values of the religion and secondly the
experience of fearing for life and limb because of the activities of an adjacent but culturally different group. When education in a religion is poor and its values are misunderstood
or set aside, it ceases to be a moral agent. It becomes instead
a badge of identity which in turn needs to be defended from
outsiders, especially when those outsiders are seen as culturally alien.

In this respect the aggression of religious fundamentalists whether Christian or Muslim arises because they are not

---

[19]   See, for example, Scott Appleby, *The Ambivalence of the Sacred* (London,
       Boulder, New York & Oxford: Rowman and Lettlefield, 2000); also,
       Michael Burleigh, *Sacred Causes: Religion and Politics from the European
       Dictators to Al Qaeda* (HarperPress, 2006).

fundamental enough. If they were, they would realise that one major implication of monotheism is that all of reality, without exception, was created by God and therefore demands our respect. In the case of any large scale monotheistic religious institution caught up in international conflict, what is required most of all both amongst the participants in the violence and those attempting to resolve it, is education in this core value. Juxtaposed with that value there needs to be a parallel investigation of the sources of violence in the personal structure of the human psyche and the socio-economic structures that perpetuate injustice, or what the liberation theologians call 'structural evil'.

Let me take the example of Christianity because I happen to have been brought to adulthood within that culture, but my choice could easily have been Islam, as I have come to understand from conversations with loving Muslim friends. It is because of the drawing together of all things under one God that the commandment to 'Love God with all your heart and mind and soul and strength' inevitably implies 'and your neighbour as yourself' and "If anyone says he loves God and hates his brother he is a liar" (1 John 4:20). [Or, as the same thought is expressed in Islam, someone who hates his neighbour is truly the enemy of Allah]. In accordance with that, the question of who is my neighbour is answered in the parable of the Good Samaritan, 'anyone I encounter who is in need'. These central values are repeated in many different ways in Jesus' Sermon on the Mount:

> Happy the gentle; they shall have the earth for their heritage
> Happy those who hunger and thirst for what is right: they shall be satisfied
> Happy are the merciful: they shall have mercy shown to them
> Happy the peacemakers: they shall be called children of God

And the golden rule,

> Always treat others as you would like them to treat you.

These precepts don't apply only to members of the in-group, as is frequently made plain by Jesus when he points to the outsider as the exemplar of love. In the parable of the Good Samaritan, it is not the officially orthodox priest and Levite who show mercy, but the despised Samaritan. These principles are extremely elementary and have their physiological correlate in the state of contemplation, in which the boundaries of the self merge into the continuum of reality. They are thus based on a human universal that is not the possession of any one religion, or even of religious believers. When we are in tune, all of us know this.

Situational violence. The code of love lies at the core of a Christian institution that nevertheless has blood on its hands, as atheist critics quite rightly point out. The same or very similar peaceable criteria for behaviour exist in the other great monotheisms, yet they too have repeatedly been embroiled in politically inspired violence against those identified as outsiders. Once these identities are set up in groups that are detached from core values, they feed into processes of alienation and potential hatred that have been studied by the social psychologist Philip Zimbardo in an investigation that was notorious for the way it turned nasty.

The Stanford Prison experiment was set up by Zimbardo in 1971.[20] He arbitrarily divided up a group of 24 volunteers and assigned them to imaginary roles as prisoners or prison guards. The situation was made as real as possible. For example the assigned prisoners were arrested by real policemen from the Palo Alto police force and then placed in a simulated prison in the basement of the Psychology Department of Stanford University in California. The arbitrarily assigned guards had their duties explained to them and Zimbardo set a two-week time boundary to see what would transpire. The horrific results are well known. After six days Zimbardo decided to halt the experiment because the hostility between guards and prisoners had become frighteningly real with the guards behaving in a brutal and sadistic way towards their charges.

Zimbardo repudiates a 'dispositional' account of the bad behaviour of the guards, pointing out that there was no rea-

---

[20] The best and simplest introduction to Philip Zimbardo's prison experiment is available on the Internet at <http://www.prisonexp.org.>

son to suppose that they were anything other than ordinary decent people when they were outside the experimental situation. Instead he proposes a 'situational' dynamic as the most important in affecting behaviour. One of the major situational factors is the strength of the boundary set up between a person's 'In-group' and all other 'Out-groups'. The sharper the boundary the more an individual may feel that hostility is legitimate. If there are other factors such as economic disputes, arguments over borders, or a long history of warfare between the parties, these all contribute to the likelihood of bad behaviour on the part of a religious group.

But why pick on religion, when scandalous behaviour is almost a permanent feature of some elements within any large organisation (e.g. the Enron scandal; US military scandal at Abu Graib, Iraq; Watergate; the persecution of religious groups in the former Soviet Union etc;)? From the perspective of secularist critics of religion the crucial difference is that whereas business, the army, and politics deal with tangible issues, religion is entirely built on stupidity and fantasy and therefore is in principle a meaningless battleground, whose rationale must in the end be power seeking for its own sake. What the sceptics are blind to is the empirical reality of the spiritual life and its centrality to any holistic solution of conflict. To summarise, when religion itself is accused of being the source of conflict it is no solution to abandon it. Violence is not caused by religion, but by human fallibility. The way forward lies within the religious context itself, in a recognition of the falling away from its heartland of relational consciousness.

Reasons for Optimism

Spirituality and social coherence. At this point I turn finally to our interplanetary visitor, and ask him if things are any better in his end of the universe. He shakes his head. Members of the species *Homo sapiens* it seems are much the same wherever they are found, inclined to be trapped by self-oriented motivation into ignoring the essence of their religion.

Yet in one crucial respect things differ on that other planet. History has not conjured up an ideology that splits off a major aspect of our biologically inbuilt awareness and calls it delusion. Because of that, the well of spiritual insight is still communally open and seen as vitally important even whilst the religious institution is recognised as fallible. Within that institution lies a vast accumulation of wisdom that runs counter to the forces that bring about social disintegration, sometimes described as the frittering away of social and spiritual capital.[21]

In the Old Testament, so often attacked for the immorality of the vengeful God depicted by some of its authors, we also discover the authentic voice of spirituality. Here is the prophet Amos, insisting that true religion is inseparable from justice and identifying the spiritually dead:

> Listen to this, you who trample on the needy and try to suppress the poor people of the country, you who say, 'When will New Moon be over so that we can sell our corn, and Sabbath, so that we can market our wheat? Then by lowering the bushel, raising the shekel, by swindling and tampering with the scales, we can buy up the poor for money and the needy for a pair of sandals, and get a price even for the sweepings of the wheat.' (Amos 8: 4–6)

Amos emphasises that it is the distancing from justice that brings with it an estrangement from spiritual awareness:

> See what days are coming — it is the Lord who speaks — days when I will bring famine on the country, a famine not of bread, a drought not of water, but of hearing the word of the Lord. They will stagger from sea to sea, wander from north to east, seeking the word of the Lord and failing to find it. (Amos 8: 11–12)

At its best the Church is a permanent and courageous reminder of our relationship to each other and of the common good, standing for Spirituality versus Alienation; Relational Consciousness versus Individualism; and Ecology versus 'The Selfish Gene'.

---

[21] See Robert Putnam's comprehensive and devastating account of the decline in social coherence in the United States, *Bowling Alone: The Collapse and Revival of American Community* (New York: Simon and Schuster, 2001).

The empirical research I have discussed in these chapters demonstrates that giving priority to individualism is a matter of choice, though in the Western world the freedom to choose is seriously compromised by its history. The assumptions of our culture encourage us to attend to one dimension of reality and ignore other equally real aspects of our biology. In effect, the culture generates psychopaths like Stirner, giving supreme authority to the awareness of themselves as isolated from the rest of reality, blind to relational consciousness and opening up a host of negative social and political consequences. As we have seen there are extremely powerful economic reasons, backed by the political establishment, for maintaining a commitment to individualism. Is it any wonder that spirituality has a difficult time and that the religious institutions are in a state of severe crisis?

Marie Dahnhart managed to escape from Stirner and in the end found her way to her convent in London. At least she had a religious institution to go to, with all its weakness. Whether that institution survives the next half-century in Western Europe must depend on how it relates to the current outburst of free-floating spirituality in the West[22] that, for my part as a practising Christian, I see as the upsurge of the Holy Spirit.

Globalization. One major reason to expect greatly increased interest in relational consciousness is the morally ambiguous phenomenon of globalisation.[23] The interlocking worldwide network of political, economic and ecological

---

[22]   In a survey I directed in 2000, 76% of the national sample claimed to have a spiritual dimension to their experience. Compared to the results of a previous survey in 1987 there was a 60% rise in report of spiritual/religious experience. Meanwhile, over approximately the same period church attendance dropped by 20%. For detailed statistics, see David Hay & Kate Hunt (2000) and for a detailed discussion, see David Hay (2006). A consultation of the latter of these two references will show that much the same pattern is to be found across most Western European nations.

[23]   For a stimulating review of the complex moral and political issues raised by globalisation, see Joseph Stiglitz's *Globalization and its Discontents* (London: Penguin Books, 2002).

systems that underlie, for example, the phenomenon of global warming, is now overwhelmingly obvious.[24] One way of imagining the complexity is to see it as a 'global brain', emphasising the importance of interrelationship and communication. The Iraq war provides another vivid and painful example of linkages that proliferate endlessly throughout world politics, via fear of international terrorism, and having material effects in fields like economics and ecology, as well as a more subtle influence on national mood and morale. We have entered what the systems theorist Ludwig von Bertalanffy calls an 'organismic' era. It requires different kinds of social, psychological and spiritual bases for experiencing and thinking through the nature of the relatedness of human beings to their 'cosmos in the mind'.

In the new global environment that affects us all, the weakness and ethical emptiness of individualism becomes obvious. One location where this is rapidly becoming clear is in the field of business management, the very area of wealth creation that Adam Smith believed was dependent upon self-interest for its functioning. The changing view can be seen especially in Third Wave industries like electronics, lasers, optics, genetics, communications, alternative energy, ocean science, space manufacture, ecological engineering, and eco-system agriculture. It is here that managers are experimenting with the idea that their role is to experience as directly as possible in the here-and-now (Donaldson's 'point mode') the business-as-a-series-of-events-in-its-environment. The process is dynamic. In the act of participation, interpretations arise that in turn lead to new insights, enlarged understanding and a fresh cycle of interpretation. Whereas in traditional mode the manager steps in with a preconceived plan to 'save' the company, in

---

[24] In what follows I am heavily dependent on the ideas of my friend and colleague Professor Gordon Lawrence who has spent many years considering the relationship between spirituality and business management. Much of his most original thought has arisen as the result of his consultancy work with members of religious congregations and the realisation that the contemplative mode is potentially highly creative in the management situation.

the ecological mode there is openness, an allowing of one-self to become aware of what is the case and in the process seeing how to go on. The closest analogy to this form of management is with contemplative prayer and it is interesting to note that these ideas have partly been drawn from the experience of consulting to religious congregations.

Similarly in the field of empirical science there is a movement away from the false detachment at one time preached as a virtue in scientific investigation. As we realise that the whole person is involved in the research act, there is a recovery of that coherence between spirituality and scientific investigation that is so manifest in the great 16th century mathematician Johannes Kepler's ecstasy when he discovered the orbits of the planets. In his Gifford Lectures in Aberdeen University during the 1950s, the eminent scientist-philosopher Michael Polanyi commented on the passage that forms the epigraph to this chapter,

> Kepler's exclamation about God having waited for him for thousands of years is a literary fancy, yet his outburst conveys a true idea of the scientific method and of the nature of science; an idea which has since been disfigured by the sustained attempt to remodel it in the likeness of a mistaken ideal of objectivity.[25]

Kepler intuitively knew that science and spirituality are not distinct from each other. In every scientific and religious endeavour fully entered into, the whole of our humanity is engaged. That insight is currently being recovered in the results of the empirical research I have been discussing. The sooner that truth is realised and the censoring out of major dimensions of our human nature is abandoned in both scientific and religious investigations, the sooner both disciplines will benefit. Spirituality will regain its rightful place at the heart of our understanding of what it is to be a true humanist.

---

[25]   Polanyi, op. cit. p. 7

References

Allport, G.W. (1962). *The Individual and His Religion,* New York: Macmillan.

Ando, J. Suzuki, A. Yamagata, S. Kijima, N. & Maekawa, H. (2004). 'Genetic and environmental structure of Cloninger's temperament and character dimensions', *Journal of Personality Disorders* 18 (4), 379–93.

Anon.(1961). *The Cloud of Unknowing,* trans. Clifton Wolters, London: Penguin Books.

APA (1994), *DSM4,* Arlington VA: American Psychiatric Publishing Inc.

Appleby, S. (2000). *The Ambivalence of the Sacred,* London, Boulder, New York & Oxford: Rowman and Littlefield Publishers.

Burleigh, M. (2006). *Sacred Causes: Religion and Politics from the European Dictators to Al Qaeda,* London: HarperPress.

Atran, S. (2002). *In Gods We Trust: The Evolutionary Landscape of Religion,* New York: Oxford University Press.

Atran, S. & Norenzayan, A. (2004). 'Religion's evolutionary landscape: counterintuition, commitment, compassion, communion', *Behavior and Brain Sciences* 27 (6), 713–30.

Aunger, R. (2001). *Darwinising Culture: the Status of Memetics as a Science,* Oxford University Press.

Azari, N.P. & Birnbacher, D. (2004). 'The role of cognition and feeling in religious experience', *Zygon* 39 (4), 901–18.

Beauregard, M. & Paquette, V. (2006). 'Neural correlates of a mystical experience in Carmelite nuns', *Neuroscience Letters* 405, 186–90.

Berman, D. (1988). *A History Of Atheism In Britain: From Hobbes To Russell,* London: Croom-Helm.

Blackmore, S. (1999). *The Meme Machine,* Oxford University Press.

Borowik, I. & Tomka, M. (eds.) (2001). *Religion and Social Change in Post-Communist Europe,* Krakow: Zakład Wydawniczy »NOMOS«

Boyer, P. (2001). *Religion Explained: The Human Instincts that Fashion Gods, Spirits and Ancestors,* London: William Heinemann.

Bremmer, J.M. (2007). 'Atheism in antiquity', in *The Cambridge Companion to Atheism* (ed. Michael Martin), Cambridge University Press.

Brown, K.C. (ed.) (1965). *Hobbes Studies*, Oxford: Blackwell.

Bruce, S. (2002). *God is Dead: Secularisation in the West*, Oxford: Blackwells.

Buber, M. (1959). *I and Thou*, (trans. Ronald Gregor Smith), Edinburgh: T & T. Clark.

Buckley, M. (1987). *At the Origins of Modern Atheism*, New Haven and London: Yale University Press.

Buckley, M. (2004). *Denying and Disclosing God: the Ambiguous Progress of Modern Atheism*, New Haven and London: Yale University Press.

Bulgakov, M. (1984). *The Master and Margarita*, London: Penguin Modern Classics.

Campbell, P.A. & McMahon, E.M. (1997). *Biospirituality: A Way to Grow*, Chicago: Loyola University Press.

Carroll, J. (1984). *Break-Out from the Crystal Palace. The Anarcho-Psychological Critique: Stirner, Neitzsche, Dostoevsky*, London and Boston: Routledge and Kegan Paul.

Carter, A. (2004). 'Of property and the human: or C.B. Macpherson, Samuel Hearne and Contemporary Theory', *University of Toronto Quarterly* 74 (3), 829–44

Casanova, J. (1994). *Public Religions in the Modern World*, Chicago University Press.

Caussade, J-P. (1971). *Self Abandonment to Divine Providence*. London: Collins/Fontana.

Chapman, J. (1959). *Spiritual Letters*, London: Sheed & Ward.

Chessick, R.D. (1999). *Emotional Illness and Creativity: A Psychoanalytic and Phenomenologic Study.* Madison: International Universities Press.

Clark, J.P. (1976). *Max Stirner's Egotism*, London: Freedom Press.

Csikszentmihalyi, I. (1988). 'Flow in a historical context: the case of the Jesuits' in Mihaly Csikszentmihalyi and Isabella Csikszentmihalyi (eds.), *Psychological Studies of Flow in Consciousness*. New York: Cambridge University Press.

Csikszentmihalyi, M. (1975). *Beyond Boredom and Anxiety*. San Francisco: Jossey-Bass.

Davie, G. (2002). *Europe the Exceptional Case: Parameters of Faith in the Modern World*, London: Darton, Longman & Todd.

D'Aquili, E. & Newberg, A. (1999). *The Mystical Mind: Probing the Biology of Religious* Experience, Minneapolis: Augsberg Press.

Dawkins, R. (1976). *The Selfish Gene*, Oxford University Press.

Dawkins, R. (2006). *The God Delusion*, London, Toronto, Sydney, Auckland and Johannesburg: Bantam Press.

Dennett, D. (2006). *Breaking the Spell: Religion as a Natural Phenomenon*, New York: Viking Penguin.

Donaldson, M. (1992). *Human Minds*, London: Allen Lane

Dreyfus, H. (1991). *Being-in-the-World*, Cambridge: MIT Press.

Durham, W. (1991). *CoEvolution: Genes, Culture and Human Destiny*, Stanford University Press.

Durkheim, É. (1897). 'Review of Antonio Labriola, *Essays on the Materialist Conception of History'*, *Revue Philosophique*, Vol. 44, pp. 646–51.

Eagleton, T. (2006). 'Review of *The God Delusion'*, in *London Review of Books*, Vol. 28 No. 20, 19 October 2006

Erlandson, D.A., Skipper, B.L. & Harris, E.L. (1993). *Doing Naturalistic Inquiry: A Guide to Methods*, Newbury Park, Cal, & London: Sage Publications, Inc.

Feuerbach, L. (1989/1841). *The Essence of Christianity*, (translated by George Eliot), Amherst, New York: Prometheus Books.

Feuerbach. L. (1967/1851). *Lectures on the Essence of Religion*. (trans. Ralph Manheim), New York & London: Harper & Row.

Gadamer, H-G. (1989). *Truth and Method*, London: Sheed and Ward.

Gardner, G. H. (1953). *Gerard Manley Hopkins, A Selection of His Poems and Prose*, Harmondsworth: Penguin.

Gendlin, E. (1981). *Focusing*, Toronto, New York, London, Sydney: Bantam Books.

Gendlin, E. (1997). *Experiencing and the Creation of Meaning: A Philosophical and Psychological Approach to the Subjective*, Evanston, Illinois: NorthWestern University Press.

Geras, N. (1983).*Marx and Human Nature: Refutation of a Legend*, London: Verso.

Gillespie, N., Cloninger, R, Heath, A. C. & Martin, N.G. (2003), 'The genetic and environmental relationship between Cloninger's dimensions of temperament and character', *Personality and Individual Differences* 35: 1931–46.

Gordon, F.M. (1976). 'The debate between Feuerbach and Stirner: an introduction', in *The Philosophical Forum*, 8, 2–3–4, reproduced on the Internet at <http://www.nonserviam.com/stirner/ reviews/ gordon.html>

Greeley, A. (1975). *The Sociology of the Paranormal: A Reconnaissance.* Sage Research Papers in the Social Sciences (Studies in Religion and Ethnicity Series No. 90–023), Beverley Hills/London: Sage Publications.

Green, A. (2006). 'Stirner and Marx', *Non Serviam #23*, April, p. 2 <http://www.nonserviam.com/magazine/issues/23.html>

Hardy, A.C. (1965). *The Living Stream*, London: Collins.

Hardy, A.C. (1966). *The Divine* Flame, London: Collins.

Harris, S. (2006) *The End of Faith: Religion, Terror and the Future of Reason*, London: Free Press.

Hay, D. (2006) *Something There: The Biology Of The Human Spirit*, London: Darton,Longman & Todd; (2007) Philadelphia: Templeton Foundation Press.

Hay D. & Hunt, K. (2000). *The Spirituality of People who don't go to Church*, Nottingham University Research Report,

Hay, D. with Nye, R. (2006). *The Spirit of the Child* (revised edition), London & Philadelphia: Jessica Kingsley Publishers.

Heidegger, M. (1962/1927). *Being and Time*, (trans. John Macquarrie & Edward Robinson), Oxford: Basil Blackwell.

Hirschman, A. (1977/1997). *The Passions and the Interests: Political Arguments for Capitalism before its Triumph*, Princeton University Press.

Hobbes, T. (1985/1651). *Leviathan* (with an introduction by C.B. Macpherson), London: Penguin Classics.

James, W. (1897). *The Will to Believe and Other Essays in Popular Philosophy*, London: Longmans, Green & Co.

James, W. (1920). *The Letters of William James*, (ed. Henry James) Boston: Little, Brown & Co.

James, W. (1985/1902). *The Varieties of Religious Experience*, Cambridge & London: Harvard University Press.

Jones, S., Martin, R. & Pilbeam, D. (eds.), (1994). *The Cambridge Encyclopedia of Human Evolution*, Cambridge University Press.

Kant, E. (1960/1793). *Religion Within the Limits of Reason Alone*, (trans. Theodore M Greene & Hoyt H. Hudson) New York: Harper & Row.

Kirk, K., Martin, N. & Eaves, L. (1999). 'Self-transcendence' as a measure of spirituality in a sample of older Australia twins', *Twin Research* 2 (2): 81–7.

Kris, E. (1988) *Psychoanalytic Explorations in Art*, Madison: International Universities Press.

Levinas, E. (1989). *The Levinas Reader* (ed. Sean Hand), Oxford: Blackwell.

Lobkowicz, N. (1969). 'Karl Marx and Max Stirner', in, Frederick J. Adelmann (ed.), *Demythologizing Marxism*, Beacon Hill: Boston College.

Locke, J.L. (1998). *Why we Don't Talk to Each Other any More: the Devoicing of Society*, New York: Simon & Schuster.

Lucas, J.R. (1997). 'Wilberforce and Huxley: A Legendary Encounter', *The Historical Journal*, Vol. 22 (2), pp. 313–30

Luria, A. (1976). *Cognitive Development: Its Cultural and Social Foundations*. (trans. Martin Lopez-Morillas and Lynn Solotaroff; ed. Michael Cole), Cambridge: Harvard University Press.

Luria, A. (2006). *The Autobiography of Alexander Luria: A Dialogue with the Making of a Mind*, Mahwah, NJ: Lawrence Erlbaum Associates.

Lynch, A. (1996). *Thought Contagion: How Belief Spreads Through Society*, New York: Basic Books.

Mackay, J.H. (2005). *Max Stirner: His Life and Work* (trans. Hubert Kennedy), Concord, California: Peremptory Publications.

Martin, R.B. (1991). *Gerard Manley Hopkins: A Very Private Life*, New York: Putnam.

Martinich, A.P. (2005). *Hobbes*, London: Routledge.

Marx, K. (1845/1998). *The German Ideology*, Amherst, New York: Prometheus Books.

McCrone, J. (1990). *The Ape that Spoke: Language and the Evolution of the Human Mind*, London: Picador.

Macpherson, C.B. (1962). *The Political Theory of Possessive Individualism*, Oxford University Press.

Monroe, K.R. (1996). *The Heart of Altruism: Perceptions of a Common Humanity*, Princeton University Press.

Muhlhausler, P. & Harré, R. (1990), *Pronouns and People*, Oxford: Blackwell.

Nagy, E. & Molnar, P. (2004). 'Homo imitans or Homo provocans? Human imprinting model of neonatal imitation'. *Infant Behavior and Development*, 27: 54–63.

Newberg, A., d'Aquili, E. & Rause, V. (2001). *Why God Won't Go Away: Brain Science and the Biology of Belief*, New York: Ballantine Books.

Newberg, A. & Iverson, G.L. (2003). 'The neural basis of the complex mental task of meditation: neurotransmitter and neurochemical considerations', *Medical Hypotheses*, 61 (2), 282–91

Newberg, A. & Waldman, M.R. (2006). *Why We Believe What We Believe: Uncovering Our Biological Need for Meaning, Spirituality, and Truth*, New York: Free Press.

Newman, S. (2001). 'Spectres of Stirner: a contemporary critique of ideology', *Journal of Political Ideologies*, 6 (1), 309-330.

Nyanaponika Thera, (1976). *The Heart of Buddhist Meditation*, Newburyport, MA: Red Wheel/Weiser.

Ong, W. (1982). *Orality and Literacy: the Technologizing of the Word*, London and New York: Routledge.

Otto, R. (1950) *The Idea of the Holy*, (2nd edn.), (trans. J.W. Harvey), Oxford: Oxford University Press.

Pascal, B. (1061). *Pascal: The Pensées*, (ed. J.M. Cohen), London: Penguin Classics.

Paterson, R.K. (1971). *The Nihilistic Egoist Max Stirner*, published for the University of Hull by Oxford University Press.

Penfield, W. & Rasmussen, T. (1950). *The Cerebral Cortex of Man : A Clinical Study of Localization of Function*, New York: Macmillan.

Polanyi, M. (1958). *Personal Knowledge: Towards a Post-Critical Philosophy*, University of Chicago Press, 1958

Preus, S. (1987). *Explaining Religion: Criticism and Theory from Bodin to Freud*, New Haven and London: Yale University Press.

Putnam, R. (2001). *Bowling Alone: The Collapse and Revival of American Community*, New York: Simon and Schuster Ltd.

QSR.NUD*IST (1996). *User's Guide*, London: Sage/SCOLARI

Sensky, T, Wilson, A., Petty, R., Fenwick, P. & Rose (1984). 'The interictal personality traits of temporal lobe epileptics: Religious belief and its association with reported mystical experiences' In R.J. Porter et al. (eds.), *Advances in Epileptology: XVth Epilepsy International Symposium* (pp. 545–9). New York: Raven Press.

Smith, A. (2000/ 1759). *The Theory of the Moral Sentiments*, Amherst New York: Prometheus Books.

Smith, A. (1999/1776). *The Wealth of Nations* (introduction by Andrew Skinner), London: Penguin Classics.

Sober, E. & Wilson, D.S. (1998). *Unto Others: The Evolution and Psychology of Unselfish Behavior*, Cambridge: Harvard University Press.

Sorell, T. (ed.) (1996) *The Cambridge Companion to Hobbes*, Cambridge University Press.

Stirner, M. (1993). *The Ego and Its Own*, (translated by Steven Byington), London: Rebel Press.

Stiglitz, J. (2002). *Globalization and its Discontents*, London: Penguin Books

Townshend, J. (2000). *C.B. Macpherson and the Problem of Liberal Democracy*, Edinburgh University Press.

Turner, J. (1986). *Without God, Without Creed: The Origins of Unbelief in America*, Baltimore: Johns Hopkins University Press.

Walzer, M. (1990). 'The communitarian critique of liberalism', *Political Theory*, 18 (1), 6-23

Watt, I. (1996). *Myths of Modern Individualism: Faust, Don Quixote, Don Juan, Robinson Crusoe*, Cambridge University Press.

Weil, S. (2001). *Waiting for God*, London: HarperCollins.

Wilde, L. (1998). *Ethical Marxism and its Radical Critics*, London: Macmillan Press.

Wilson, B. (1966). *Religion in Secular Society*, London: C.A. Watts.

Wilson, D.S. (2002). *Darwin's Cathedral: Evolution, Religion and the nature of society*, University of Chicago Press.

Wordsworth, W. (1990). *Wordsworth: The Poems* (ed. John O. Hayden), London: Penguin.

Wuthnow, R. (1976). *The Consciousness Reformation*. Berkeley: University of California Press.

Zimbardo, P. (2007). Webpage on the Internet at <http://www.prisonexp.org.>

Zizioulas, J. (2004). *Being as Communion*, London: Darton, Longman & Todd.

Index

SOCIETAS: essays in political and cultural criticism

Public debate has been impoverished by two competing trends
On the one hand the trivialization of the media means that in-depth commentary has given way to the ten second soundbite. On the other hand the explosion of knowledge has increased specialization, and academic discourse is no longer comprehensible.

This was not always so — especially for political debate. But in recent years the tradition of the political pamphlet has declined. However the introduction of the digital press makes it possible to re-create a more exciting age of publishing. *Societas* authors are all experts in their own field, but the essays are for a general audience. The books are available retail at the price of £8.95/$17.90 each, or on bi-monthly subscription for only £5/$10. Details at **imprint-academic.com/societas**

IMPRINT ACADEMIC, PO Box 200, Exeter, EX5 5YX, UK
Tel: (0)1392 851550   Fax: (0)1392 851178   sandra@imprint.co.uk